SCREEN PLAY

GEORGE SULLIVAN

SCREEN PLAY

The Story of Video Games

Frederick Warne · New York · London

150

COPYRIGHT ACKNOWLEDGMENTS

Text copyright © 1983 by George Sullivan
All rights reserved. No part of this book may be reproduced or transmitted in any form or by any means without permission in writing from the publisher, except for brief quotations used in connection with reviews written specifically for inclusion in a magazine or newspaper.
Frederick Warne & Co., Inc.
New York, New York
Library of Congress Cataloging in Publication Data
Sullivan, George, 1927–
Screen play.
Includes index.
Summary: Traces the development of video games since 1966 when an electronics engineer named Ralph Baer invented and marketed the Odyssey home game system.
1. Video games—History—Juvenile literature.
[1. Video games—History. 2. Electronic games—History. 3. Games—History] I. Title.
GV1469.3.S94   1983   794.8'2   83–10606
ISBN 0–7232–6251–9 (cloth)
ISBN 0-7232-6254-3 (paper)
Printed in the U.S.A. by Haddon Craftsmen
Book design by Camilla Filancia
1 2 3 4 5 87 86 85 84 83 (c)
1 2 3 4 5 87 86 85 84 83 (p)

ACKNOWLEDGMENTS

Many people were helpful to me in providing background information and photographs for use in this book. Special thanks are offered to Ginny Juhnke, Karen Esler, and Jamie Pinto, at Atari; Margaret Davis, at Imagic; Connie Stewart, at Intel; Barbara Wruck, at Coleco Industries; Kathy Kennedy, at Intellivision; Dona Bailey, at Videa, and Jesse Sudradjat, at Ralph Silver Associates.

Special thanks are also due Richard Mansfield, Senior Editor, *Compute!* magazine, for permission to reprint the computer programs that appear in Chapter 6. The author is also grateful to Joe Claro, Editor, *Blip;* Steve Epstein, Broadway Arcade, New York City; Francesca Kurti, at T.L.C. Studios; Dr. Lewis Steingesser; Aime LaMontagne, Jr.; Don Wigal; Steve Bloom; Merrilee Jo Newman; and Jose Matamales.

GEORGE SULLIVAN

CONTENTS

"New York loves video games" a sign proclaims outside one of the city's arcades. (George Sullivan)

1. Revolution

Checkers originated in the twelfth century in Europe, probably in the south of France. The Romans are said to have been the first to have gambled with dice. Chess was played about as early as the seventh century. Board games have been traced to ancient Crete. But recently, the art of game playing was completely revolutionized. Instead of one person opposing another in an activity involving skill or chance, it's now possible for a player to oppose a computer, and the game action unfolds on a television screen. The era of video games is here.

The games are everywhere. The type that stands about six feet tall, boasts a 19-inch screen, and comes to life when a quarter or a token is inserted can be found in supermarkets, bowling alleys, bakeries, laundromats, pizza parlors, delicatessens, airline terminals, train and bus stations, and department stores. They are known as coin-operated games, or coin-ops for short.

As these tokens attest, games are popular from coast to coast. (Van Brook of Lexington, Inc.)

Coin-ops can also be found in game arcades. What is an arcade? In *Play Meter* magazine, an industry trade publication, an arcade is defined as any location having coin-operated entertainment—including pinball machines and jukeboxes—that offers ten or more video games. Your neighborhood candy store, which may provide only two or three video games, is not an arcade. It's what the industry calls a "street location."

By the early 1980s, more than one million game consoles were in operation. (Aime LaMontagne. Tron is a trademark of Walt Disney Productions and licensed by Bally-Midway Mfg. Co.)

A recent survey conducted by *Play Meter* found that there were about 1 ½ million video games in operation in approximately 24,000 arcades and 400,000 street locations. When you insert 25 cents or a token in a coin-operated game, you may have to defend yourself against enemy spaceships, ferocious robots, or rocket-firing tanks. Or maybe you'll guide a yellow disk through a maze of pathways while evading pursuing monsters, or rescue a pretty maiden who is being held captive by a nasty gorilla.

Electronic-monster visitors from outer space and the other game characters have also invaded the American home. On nearly 20 million television sets people play Ms. Pac-Man or Tron rather than watch situation comedies or hour-long detective shows. Someday, according to industry experts, approximately half of the nation's television sets will be equipped with plug-in video game systems.

These game systems are made up of hardware and software. The hardware is the console into which the cartridge—or software—is inserted. The console takes the form of a rectangular box, about a foot wide, a little more

---

About 20 million of the nation's TV sets can be tuned in to play games. (Atari, Inc.)

than a foot in length, and several inches high. It attaches to the back of any home television set through an adapter that screws into the VHF aerial terminals.

The game cartridges are inserted into the console. Each cartridge is about the size of a package of cigarettes. When you want to play a different game, you merely replace one cartridge with another.

Games can also be brought into the home through the telephone. This service, called GameLine, allows owners of most game consoles to tap a central computerized library of video games on a pay-per-play basis. A unique device, called a Master Module, calls the GameLine central computer on the owner's telephone line, receives the video-game program, stores it in its memory unit, and then permits the game to be played just as if it were a standard cartridge for that game.

Video games can also be played on home computers. Special cartridges are required. Game programs for computers equipped with disk drive are available on magnetic floppy disks.

The hundreds of different games available for home systems have a greater diversity than those found in arcades. Besides the combat and space games, the skill and adventure games, home-video enthusiasts can also choose baseball, basketball, football, and other sports, plus such classics as chess, checkers, and backgammon.

GameLine System, a product of Control Video Corporation (CVC), allows owners of game consoles to receive games via home telephone lines.

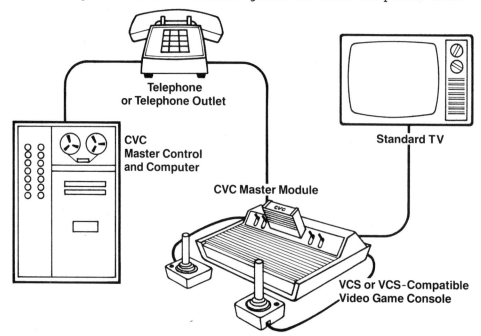

Telephone
or Telephone Outlet

CVC
Master Control
and Computer

Standard TV

CVC Master Module

VCS or VCS-Compatible
Video Game Console

Young children get instruction in addition and subtraction. (Andy Levin Children's Computer Workshop)

Not all video-game software is meant merely to entertain. Some software is educational. From Atari, the number-one company in home video games, has come Hangman, a word game in which players fill in blanks between letters, and Concentration, in which players match up hidden familiar objects. Several software manufacturers also sell the basics of computer language and programming in cartridge form. Atari, in cooperation with the Children's Computer Workshop, has available a series of educational games for children in the three-to-seven age group. The games are meant to aid in developing a child's ability to recognize letters and numbers and his or her sense of direction and timing. To play the games, which feature such noted television favorites as Big Bird and the Cookie Monster, Atari has designed a special oversize controller that is simpler for preschoolers to handle and operate. Intellivision, one of Atari's chief rivals, has created educational games titled Math Fun and Word Fun. ColecoVision involves the Smurfs in cartoony "play-and-learn" games.

All that has happened in the video-game industry has occurred in a very short time. The concept of using the home TV screen for game playing began in 1966, the year the idea occurred to Ralph Baer, a Manchester, New Hampshire, electronics engineer.

In the early 1970s Nolan Bushnell developed the first coin-op game to catch the public eye. The success of coin-operated games in turn triggered a boom in the sales of home systems. By 1982, according to an article in *The New York Times,* arcade and home games formed a $7-billion-a-year industry. In comparison, Hollywood at the time was selling a little over $3 billion worth of tickets to the American moviegoers each year.

What has occurred in recent years as far as video games are concerned typifies the technological revolution that is sweeping America. Some people say that it is a change as profound as the Industrial Revolution of the eighteenth century, which caused millions of workers to be driven off farms and into factories.

Video games are but one small part of this revolution. Overall it is evidenced by a shift from heavy industries—steel, auto, glass, rubber, and the like—to high-technology, or high-tech, industries. This new frontier includes the telecommunications, robotics, and aerospace industries. It also takes in semiconductor and computer manufacturers to be discussed later. You have lived through much of the revolution. The advances it has triggered will affect your life in a thousand different ways.

2. How Games Work

It wasn't many years ago that California's Santa Clara Valley, a wide swath of rolling-hill land about an hour's drive south of San Francisco, was quiet and obscure farm country. The farmers grew apricots, plums, and cherries, and they produced about half of the world's dried prunes. "The Valley of Heart's Delight" is what the chamber of commerce called it.

All that has changed. Bulldozers began rumbling across the orchards in the 1950s and they haven't stopped yet. Tens of thousands of acres of fruit trees have been replaced by scores of campuslike industrial parks where more than a thousand high-technology companies pour out electronic devices that have revolutionized our lives.

The low rectangular concrete buildings that house these companies are surrounded by carefully tended lawns and clusters of small shrubs, and all have big parking lots. Most of the companies have high-tech sounding names—Intel, Cemetak, Syntex, Calma, Control Data, Zilog, Digetel, Siliconics, and Koltron.

Atari's headquarters, one of about fifty buildings the company occupies in Silicon Valley, is typical of design and construction in the area. (George Sullivan)

Today, the Santa Clara Valley is known as Silicon Valley. The companies located there are developing and exploiting new uses for the microprocessor chip, the brains and basic building block of virtually every piece of modern electronic equipment, video games included.

The term Silicon Valley became popular because silicon, a rock-hard, silver-gray material found in common beach sand is one of the chief materials used in making microprocessor chips. Silicon forms the base upon which the thin films of electronic components are etched to form the chip circuitry.

A microprocessor chip is what makes a pocket calculator work. It's what endows a cash register with the ability to total bills and keep inventories up to date. Microprocessors tune in radios, pump gas, and control the operation of some car engines. It's microprocessors that have made possible home computers. A microprocessor serves as the "boss" chip in Donkey Kong and Tron, and Zaxxon and Dig Dug. It's what empowers Mario, at your command, to jump over a barrel that threatens to flatten him. It counts your shots as you fire at the Zaxxon robot, and after you've put six of them on target, it rewards you by destroying it.

The development of the microprocessor dates back to the late 1940s, when scientists at the Bell Telephone Laboratories discovered semiconductors—such substances as germanium, and later silicon, through which the flow of electricity could be easily increased or decreased. They were called semi—or "half"—conductors because their ability to conduct electrical impulses was less than that of a good conductor such as copper, but greater than that of an insulator such as glass.

The semiconductor led to the development of the transistor (short for transfer resistance), a sandwich of semiconducting materials. The transistor was invented in 1947, also at Bell Labs. Soon tiny transistors were used to replace bulky glass vacuum tubes that amplified and controlled electric currents in radios, early television sets, and the first computers. They could move electricity tens of thousands of times faster than vacuum tubes and with far fewer failures. Transistor radios began to appear in the late 1950s. Transistors were first used in the manufacture of television sets during the 1960s.

Transistors had a startling effect upon computers. The first electronic digital computer in the United States, introduced to the general public by means of a demonstration at the University of Pennsylvania in 1946, was a collection of 18,000 vacuum tubes, 70,000 resistors, 10,000 capicitors, and 6,000 switches. It occupied the space of a two-car garage. Today's home computer is about the size of an office typewriter.

Marcian "Ted" Hoff headed the project team that developed the first microprocessor. (Courtesy Intel Corporation)

The transistor had one failing, however. It sometimes chipped from its circuit board, the plastic card upon which its snakelike wires were mounted.

This problem was solved by etching a number of transistors directly onto a slice of silicon and providing connections between them. The integrated circuit (IC) had been born. By 1969 engineers at Intel, a Silicon Valley company formed the year before, developed a process that enabled them to integrate thousands of transistors onto a small chip of silicon.

From the large-scale integrated circuit, it was a short step to the microprocessor, the so-called computer on a chip. The very first microprocessor was developed by an Intel project team headed by Marcian (Ted) Hoff. Intended for use by a Japanese company that manufactured calculators, it was introduced in November 1971 and contained 2,300 transistors.

In the years that followed, engineers learned to cram more and more transistors onto individual chips. A chip with 5,000 transistors could control a digital watch; 20,000, a pocket calculator; and 100,000, a home computer.

Intel's 4004, the first microprocessor chip, was introduced in November 1971. It contained 2300 transistors. (Courtesy Intel Corporation)

The microprocessors used in video games are called dedicated microprocessors. They have been designed to do only one type of job, and you cannot change them.

The dedicated microprocessor is what makes the video game different from a computer. With a video game, you're always "playing" a program written by someone else. With a computer, however, you can write programs that will be executed by the machine.

Besides the microprocessor, there are six basic elements that make up a video game. This is true whether it is an arcade game or one that is played on a home console. The six elements are:

1. **Input.** This is what you, the player, communicate in terms of instructions to the game's central processing unit. You usually do this by means of a joystick, paddles, or a keyboard.

2. **Memory.** A microprocessor cannot hold all of the data the operation of a game requires, so memory chips help out. A video game has two types of memory:

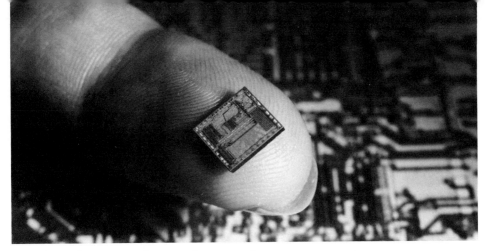

The first chip, in a classic photograph. (Courtesy Intel Corporation)

This microprocessor, which first appeared in 1982, contained 128,000 transistors in a square chip of silicon that measured only one-third inch on each side. (Courtesy Intel Corporation)

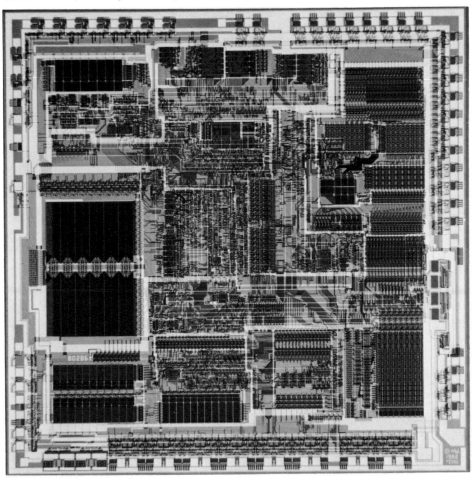

Integrated circuits are designed and plotted by computer programmers on a special computer. The circuits, once designed, are transferred to a silicon chip. (Atari, Inc.)

(a) One is called Read Only Memory, or ROM. Here the computer stores the information upon which the game is based. In Pac-Man, for instance, it is ROM that makes the game Pac-Man and not Donkey Kong or Q*Bert. ROM draws the maze outlines, the dots, energizers, the monsters, and Pac-Man himself. From ROM you get the game's *wukka-wukka* sound. In home video games the cartridges are always ROM. Each contains the game's instructions and all the special symbols and sounds that are necessary to it. If you were an electronics expert and could take a close-up look at the circuitry of a cartridge, you would see that all of its switches have been fused either open or shut. In other words, the play of the game is fixed; you cannot make any changes.

(b) The second type of memory is Random Access Memory, or RAM. RAM is temporary memory. It gives you the score, the day's high scores, the initials of the high scorers, and the number of men or "lives" you have remaining at any given time. RAM chips lose their memory when the power is lost. For example, when the owner of an arcade wants to erase the table containing the game's high scores, all he has to do is unplug the machine. When he plugs it back in, the chart is all zeroes. RAM is like writing on a blackboard. What's there can easily be erased once it's been read. By contrast, ROM is something like a book of instructions. You can consult it anytime you wish and it never changes.

3. **The Central Processing Unit.** This is a single microchip that controls the overall functioning of the game. The CPU executes your in-

structions in accordance with the information contained in the game's ROM and RAM. The CPU also sees to it that the results get to the output point —the screen—so you know exactly what is going on. All of this happens at an incredible rate of speed. The CPU in a video game is capable of executing some 500,000 elementary mathematical instructions *per second*. (Components in sophisticated computers can handle up to 10 billion commands per second.)

4. **Arithmetic Logic Unit (ALU).** The ALU is where the information is sorted, calculations performed, and instructions executed.

5. **Output.** This is the information that appears on the screen after the game's various other elements have processed the input. What you see on the screen is the result of your instructions being translated into a sequence of electrical signals. These signals are sent to an electron "gun" that is housed in a vacuum tube behind the video screen. The gun fires bursts of electrons at the screen's back surface. The electrons strike zillions of tiny bits of phosphor that coat the screen, energizing them. These minute dots combine to form the images you see. This process is known as raster graphics. Most video games rely on raster.

Some games, however, are programmed with vector graphics. In vector display, a vector draws lines from one point to another. The lines form

---

Circuitry from Intellivision's **NBA Basketball** cartridge (*left*) features two ROM chips, each contained within rectangular housing. **The circular components are capacitors.** (George Sullivan)

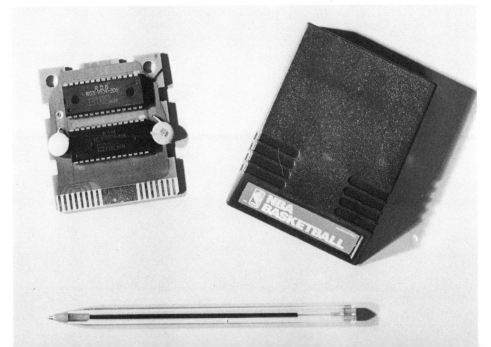

sharp, brilliant geometric shapes that often have a three-dimensional quality. Asteroids was the first well-known game to use vector graphics. Full-color vector graphics are provided in Tempest and Eliminator. Vectrex, the home video game system from General Consumer Electronics, also makes use of vector graphics. Incidentally, Vectrex doesn't have to be hooked up to a home television screen. It contains its own 9-inch black-and-white monitor, and special cartridges are available for the systems.

The Vectrex game system relies on vector graphics. (George Sullivan)

6. **The Bus.** In any game, the ROM, the RAM, the Arithmetic Logic Unit, and other parts of the game are connected to the microprocessor and to one another by a system of electrical pathways. These circuits are known collectively as the bus.

How do all of these elements work together? Suppose you're playing a space game in which you control the movement of a spaceship by means of a joystick and fire a laser gun with a firing button. The RAM allows you to move the spaceship and fire the laser when you want and in the direction of your choosing—as long as your choices conform to what's stored in the ROM.

Suppose you press the laser's firing button. Switches fly into position ordering a laser burst to be "painted" at the spot you've selected. Other switches signal the sound of a laser burst to be heard. If the microprocessor detects a coincidence in the aiming of the laser and the target at which you've aimed, it dips into the ROM and orders up an explosion. It then makes the appropriate adjustment in the score.

When you move the joystick, you are again sending signals to the microprocessor. The joystick works like a pointer on a scale. Each number to which it points adjusts switches that control the spaceship's position. The setting is translated to a sequence of electronic signals. The signals are sent to the electronic gun behind the video screen, and the gun fires bursts of electrons that light up a pattern of dots in the screen phosphor. The dots form the image of your spaceship.

This all takes place at an incredible rate of speed. When you push the joystick to move the spaceship to a new position, the microprocessor is actually making the spaceship disappear and is redrawing it completely 30 times a second!

If a game's characters, in accordance with the game's ROM and RAM, always acted in the same way, you could memorize their patterns and learn to anticipate their movements. You could learn to beat the game. Game manufacturers try to prevent this with a device called the Random Event Generator, or REG. The REG keeps you guessing. If you've played Pac-Man, you're sure to have noticed that there are times the monsters follow you doggedly. You're then able to "eat" an energizer, devouring two or three of them without any difficulty. But other times, the monsters suddenly stop following you and retreat. Such unpredictable movement is evidence of the Random Event Generator at work.

Manufacturers can also change the game's play by simply changing the game's electronics. When Pac-Man was first introduced, the monsters moved quite slowly. But as players got better and better and were able to keep playing the game for longer periods, the game was changed to speed up the monsters' movements. In fact, the experienced players could tell at a glance whether a particular game was a fast game or a slow game.

Pac-Man specialists also learned to beat the game through pattern play —that is, by memorizing a route that Pac-Man could take which would enable him to consume all the dots and energizers. When the manufacturers of the game realized what had happened, they designed new patterns for Pac-Man. And when players memorized these, they redesigned the game a second and later a third time. The last change was effected by the addition of a single chip.

About all of today's arcade games are subject to such modification. When, for example, Atari released Food Fight in the 1980s, it was sold with a kit of electronic parts that enabled the arcade operator to adjust the number of "lives" that could be applied to Charlie Chuck, the game's chief character. The owner could also adjust the game's bonus-level settings.

Video games have come so far so fast that even the companies that manufacture them have been taken by surprise. Take the case of Atari's Video Computer System. It was originally created to offer only two types of games: paddle games, or Pong and its offspring, and tank-battle games. Today, of course, an enormous quantity and variety of games can be played on the VCS.

Games available today represent a tremendous improvement over what was being sold a few years ago. The color and sound are better. The games themselves are much more exciting and challenging. This is largely because engineers have been able to make transistors smaller and smaller while putting more and more of them on a single chip. By 1990, it's said, the engineers will be able to squeeze 10 million transistors on a chip that is less than half the size of a postage stamp. That chip would make some game!

3. Video-Game Pioneer

Popular Electronics magazine called him the "Thomas Edison of the home TV game." To *Videography* and several other publications, he is the "father of the video game." In 1980, when the New York Patent Law Association named him Inventor of the Year, a spokesperson for the organization referred to him as "Mr. Television Games."

His name is Ralph Baer. In more than three decades as an electronics engineer—mostly for Sanders Associates of Nashua, New Hampshire— Baer received over sixty worldwide patents, most of them relating to video games. Many of today's video games are produced under license to his patents.

One of Baer's first patents is probably the most important of them all. Filed on August 10, 1970, it bears patent number 3,829,095. It concerns "an apparatus and method . . . for the generation, display, and manipulation of symbols upon the screens of television receivers for the purpose of training simulation, playing games and for engaging in other activities by one or more participants."

At the time that Baer first hit upon the idea of using the screens of home television sets for game playing, Nolan Bushnell, the founder of Atari and the individual often identified with the beginnings of the video-game industry, was only a sophomore at the University of Utah. Nobody had even dreamed of Intellivision, ColecoVision, or any of the other home game systems popular today. Baer's story is one of hard work and dedication. But more than that, he had the ability to take an enormous store of technical knowledge he had acquired over the years and use that knowledge in a highly original way.

Baer, his father, mother, and a sister, fleeing from Nazi Germany, arrived in New York in 1938. Baer went to work in a small New York leather

Ralph Baer in the workshop of his Manchester, New Hampshire, home.
(George Sullivan)

factory. He was sixteen years old. One day a friend of his sister's came to the Baer home in the Bronx, bringing a copy of *Cosmopolitan* with her. When Ralph thumbed through the magazine, an advertisement with the headline "Make Big Money in Radio" caught his eye.

The advertisement, placed by the National Radio Institute, offered learn-by-mail lessons in radio repair. Ralph signed up for the course. Not long after, he landed a job as a radio serviceman. When television was introduced to the American public in the years before World War II, Ralph learned to repair TV sets, too.

After serving in England and France with a Military Intelligence unit during the war, Ralph returned home to enter the American Television Institute of Technology in Chicago, becoming, as he once put it, "one of the first people ever to earn a bachelor's degree in TV engineering." After he graduated, Ralph returned to New York and worked as an electrical engineer. In 1959 he joined Sanders Associates, a Nashua company that was to become deeply involved in the development of advanced technology electronics systems and products.

Married by now, and the father of two sons and a daughter, Baer and his family lived in Manchester, New Hampshire. He had been with Sanders only a short time when he was named to head the company's equipment design division.

Baer had long puzzled over the thought of what one might be able to do with home television besides turn it on, watch a program, and turn it off. He recognized that a TV set was a complex piece of electronic equipment. And there it was, stationed in about 60 million homes.

One day in 1966, while waiting for a friend at the East Side Airline Terminal in New York, the idea came to him. You could use all those TV sets for playing games. When he got back to his office in New Hampshire, Baer wrote out a detailed description of his idea. The memorandum, dated September 1, 1966, was eight pages in length.

"The purpose of the invention," Baer wrote, "is to provide a large variety of low-cost data entry devices which can be used by an operator to communicate with a monochrome or color TV set of standard commercial, unmodified type. Entry to the TV set is to be gained either through direct connection to the video system or by connection to the antenna terminals." If you have a video game system in your home today, Baer's memo, written in 1966, pretty much describes it.

Baer went on to describe several types of games that might be used with the system. There were to be action games, in which the skill of the operator was to play a part; instructional games, designed to teach the basics of a variety of subjects; and artistic games, wherein the player manipulated controls to produce basic designs. Perhaps the latter idea was a forerunner of Qix, an arcade game introduced in 1981 in which the player drew straight lines to claim territory. Board games and card games were others that Baer's description included.

At the time, Baer was supervising some 500 engineers and other technicians at Sanders Associates. It was not the type of job that gave him much spare time for creating video-game hardware.

Nevertheless, before the end of 1966, Baer had managed to build a primitive system that produced two spots that chased one another around the screen of a black-and-white TV set. The success of his experiment increased his optimism. When he told company officials what he had achieved, they shared his enthusiasm. Money and space was provided for additional research.

Two other engineers—Bill Harrison and Bill Rusch—were hired to work

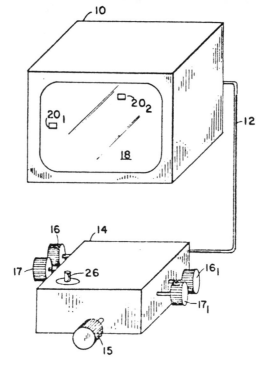

Baer's patent drawings for a "Television Gaming and Training Apparatus." (Ralph Baer)

full-time on the project. They moved into a tiny enclosed office, which was packed with a work bench, two desks, and stacks of electronic equipment. Baer would pop in and out as often as he could to see how the project was moving along. "It was my hobby shop," he said. The door to the lab was kept locked at all times. Only Baer, Harrison, and Rusch had keys. Rumors began to circulate throughout the company about what was going on in *that* room.

The three men made rapid progress. By the early months of 1967 they had a basic ball-and-paddle game working. By September of that year they had completed a hockey game which was quite sophisticated, for the speed of the electronic puck depended on how hard you hit it. The trio also developed several chase games.

At this point there were still no microprocessor chips available to Baer and his colleagues. They hadn't been invented yet. And integrated circuits were so expensive that he didn't consider using them. In other words, the technology that was being spawned in Silicon Valley didn't concern Baer. He was pursuing his own course. It was something like building an automobile, disregarding the gasoline engine, and ending up with a big sail to make it go.

"I put the whole thing together with about 40 diodes [a diode is a semiconductor through which current can pass in only one direction] and 40 transistors," Baer said. "What that gave us was a line down the middle of the screen to indicate the net, paddles, and a ball."

Early in 1968 Baer began applying for patents on his invention. These patents, once they were granted, gave Sanders Associates the exclusive right to make, use, and sell video ball-and-paddle games. Such games are available from many different companies today, but only because they have been licensed by Sanders to manufacture and sell them.

Once Baer felt assured that his idea was practical, his next task was to find a company to market it. He and his associates agreed that a major consumer electronics company would be best suited for the job. During the early months of 1969 Baer demonstrated the system for representatives of RCA, Zenith, General Electric, Magnavox, and several other firms. Eventually, Magnavox agreed to manufacture and distribute it. Odyssey was the name that Magnavox chose for the system. It went on sale in 1972. The Odyssey system that began showing up in stores that fall closely followed Baer's original concepts as outlined in his early memo. It consisted of a game console that could be attached to any standard TV set, black-and-white or color.

But unlike the present day, when you must buy game cartridges after

Advertisement for the first Odyssey system.

you've purchased a console, the original Odyssey included twelve different plug in games printed on circuit cards. Table Tennis, Tennis, Football, and Ski were among them; Submarine, Haunted House, Cat and Mouse, and Roulette were some of the others. If you wanted to play Haunted House, you inserted a printed circuit card programmed with the Haunted House game into a slot in the front of the console. The game's printed circuit cards, all of which had been designed by Baer, were simple versions of the game cartridges of today. But in addition to inserting a circuit card into the console, you had to attach the appropriate plastic overlay to the TV screen. The overlay provided the background for the game you were to play—a green table and net for Table Tennis, a rink and goals for Hockey, a ramshackle old house for Haunted House, and so on.

"It would have been too expensive to provide game backgrounds electronically," Baer explained. "The plastic overlays were the solution." Baer also found it too costly to provide electronic scoring. Players were provided a small cardboard scoreboard upon which they could keep track of points, downs, plays, quarters, and other such information.

As an optional purchase, Odyssey owners were offered a Shooting Gallery for $39.95. (The Odyssey system itself cost about $100.) This included circuit cards, plastic overlays, and an electronic rifle for four different games. The games were Shootout, Dogfight, Prehistoric Safari, and Shooting Gallery. If two players decided to play Dogfight, which pitted a World War I flying ace against the Red Baron, one player would assume the role of the ace and would be equipped with the rifle. The opposing player was the Red Baron and controlled a small white light on the screen,

The original Odyssey system offered twelve different games, each with a printed circuit card. Six of those cards are shown in the foreground here.

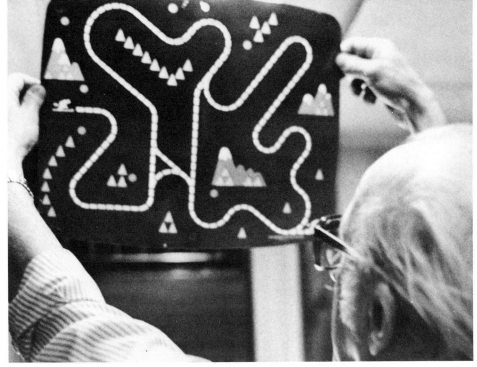

A plastic overlay for each game had to be fitted over the TV screen. Ralph Baer displays the overlay for Odyssey's skiing game. (George Sullivan)

which was the target. The electronic circuitry within the rifle barrel was sensitive to the light on the screen. The player armed with the rifle would take a position about six feet from the screen, aim at the light, and pull the trigger. If he or she had aimed accurately, the light would disappear. The opposing player would then establish the light in a new position.

One flaw in the game was that the light on the screen could also be extinguished by pointing the rifle barrel at *any* light source, such as a lamp or the sun's rays. Shooting-gallery games were best played in a darkened room.

For a new product, the Odyssey game system sold well. About 85,000 units were purchased in 1972 (and about 20,000 electronic rifles). But consumers got the mistaken notion from television commercials that Odyssey games could be played only on Magnavox television sets. Sales went downhill in the years that followed. Odyssey was also battered by competition during the late 1970s, which was a direct result of technological advances that were taking place.

In 1975 the General Instrument Corporation, in a plant operated by the company in Glenrothes, Scotland, developed a microprocessor chip that

SHOOTING GALLERY TARGETS

. . . offers you an exciting new dimension in the enjoyment of your ODYSSEY game simulator. Your SHOOTING GALLERY includes the ELECTRONIC RIFLE, two Printed Circuit Game Cards and 4 different Game Overlays in two sizes. The total unit offers six variations for testing your skill!

ELECTRONIC RIFLE

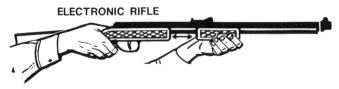

An electronic shooting gallery was also available to Odyssey owners.

---

contained much of the circuitry required for playing home video games. Called the AY 3-8500, the chip was inexpensive, costing game manufacturers only $5 or $6.

Besides providing the basic ball and paddle game, the chip had circuits for tennis, soccer, and squash. In each of these games the speed and rebound angle of the ball could be easily controlled. The chip also provided automatic scoring.

"The chip enabled video-game manufacturers to develop games of far greater variety and complexity," said Ralph Baer. "No longer did you have

---

A schematic diagram of the AY 3-8500 chip showing the functions it provided. (Ralph Baer)

Top View

• NC ⊏ ●1	28 ⊐ NC •
V_{SS} (Ground) ⊏ 2	27 ⊐ Hit Input
Sound Output ⊏ 3	26 ⊐ Shot Input
V_{CC} ⊏ 4	25 ⊐ Reset Input
Ball Angles ⊏ 5	24 ⊐ Score and Field Output
Ball Output ⊏ 6	23 ⊐ Practice
Ball Speed ⊏ 7	22 ⊐ Squash
Manual Serve ⊏ 8	21 ⊐ Soccer
Right Player Output ⊏ 9	20 ⊐ Tennis
Left Player Output ⊏ 10	19 ⊐ Rifle Game 2
Right Bat Input ⊏ 11	18 ⊐ Rifle Game 1
Left Bat Input ⊏ 12	17 ⊐ Clock Input
Bat Size ⊏ 13	16 ⊐ Sync Output
• NC ⊏ 14	15 ⊐ NC •

to be content with simply moving little rectangles around. You could put a playing field up there, display scores, and provide neat sounds."

Coleco Industries was the first company to take advantage of the General Instrument chip, offering a game called Telstar in 1976. It consisted of a console with two control knobs and a switch that allowed the player to select a ball-and-paddle game, tennis, or soccer.

Coleco, incidentally, is an acronym that stands for Connecticut Leather Company. When the company's founder, Maurice Greenberg, a Russian

Coleco's Telstar, introduced in 1976. (George Sullivan)

Telstar's simple circuitry. The **AY 3-8500** chip is at the upper lefthand **corner.** (George Sullivan)

immigrant from Minsk, set up shop in 1932 on Market Street in Hartford, Connecticut, he sold rubber heels and soles to shoe-repair shops. The company began branching out in the 1940s, selling leathercraft kits, and later, above-ground wading and swimming pools. By the 1980s Coleco was one of the most innovative companies in the video-game field.

With Coleco's Telstar, you could hit the ball slow or fast, make it travel straight or curve, or rebound it at either wide or narrow angles. The public loved Telstar and orders poured in. Coleco expanded production and began introducing similar and newer games. And other companies followed Coleco's example.

Fairchild Instrument and Camera Corporation was the first company to introduce a truly programmable video-game system. The Fairchild unit, which began showing up in the stores late in 1976, offered built-in hockey and tennis games. More important, it possessed the ability to accept a stream of new cartridges as they were developed—cartridges for playing blackjack, baseball, football, and more than a dozen other games.

Each Fairchild console used a single microprocessor chip, plus four semiconductor random access memory units. It had a dependable, easy-to-use hand controller. But after about 300,000 units were sold, Fairchild decided it didn't want to be in the video-game business anymore. Zircon International, Inc., took over the system.

RCA followed Fairchild into the market, introducing a black-and-white game system in 1977. Black-and-white video games were received with about the same enthusiasm as rain at a picnic. The RCA venture was a fiasco and the company abandoned it. National Semiconductor in 1977 introduced a three-game home system, also on one chip, but faded from the scene not long after.

Still another home system, Astrocade, was introduced in 1978. The Atari Video Computer System, or VCS (profiled in the next chapter), which came to dominate that field, and Mattel's Intellivision, were also launched before the end of the decade.

Magnavox attempted a comeback in 1978, offering Odyssey^2, a system that took advantage of the new chip technology. Thanks to the chip, Magnavox, like the other companies, was able to eliminate cardboard scoreboards and TV screen overlays for game backgrounds. By the 1980s Magnavox (which by then had been acquired by the North American Philips Consumer Electronics Corporation), held down fourth place in the home game field, behind Atari, Intellivision, and ColecoVision.

All that happened in the video-game field during the 1970s and into the 1980s was a boon to Ralph Baer. He was able to live in very comforta-

With the introduction of Odyssey², Magnavox was able to eliminate screen overlays and cardboard scoreboards.

ble circumstances, although he did not become a wealthy man. "It gave me a lot of freedom," he said. "When it all began, I was working twelve to fourteen hours a day, supervising hundreds of engineers and support personnel. I was a technical administrator. But when the license money started coming in, it made a difference. Now I'm back in development work and I can come and go as I please. I like that."

Baer made good use of his freedom. During the late 1970s and early 1980s, he was granted more than 30 patents for inventions relating to video games. Most of these looked toward the future of games, home computers, and video disks. Tomorrow's game player, Baer says, "might use a video disk to guide his Star Fighter against attacking enemy spacecraft, or might be found driving 50 laps of the Indianapolis Speedway."

Using video disks to produce realistic effects creates technical problems, Baer points out, problems in synchronizing the disks and the game play, and in passing large quantities of computer data back and forth. Solving such problems occupied much of Baer's time during the 1980s.

Baer was once asked what his reaction was in seeing the idea he had conceived in 1966 grow into a giant entertainment industry, one that came to outstrip the movies and records in terms of annual sales.

"The whole thing was totally unforeseeable," he said. "Absolutely unforeseeable." Then he added with a grin, "But I did foresee a lot."

4. King Pong

At approximately the same time that Ralph Baer and his colleagues were developing the first home video-game system, arcade games were getting started, too. Their development followed an entirely different path.

As early as 1962 Steve Russell, a graduate student at the Massachusetts Institute of Technology in Cambridge, Massachusetts, wrote a computer program for a game called Spacewar. It offered two dots that represented spacecraft, each of which was controlled by a separate lever. There was also a torpedo button for each which, when pressed, would cause the spaceship to emit a burst of light, destroying the enemy.

Remember, this was 1962. Computers of that time were huge machines costing millions of dollars. They were so big they had to be housed in specially constructed rooms and so complex it took a staff of attendants to operate them. Most computers then were found on college campuses.

That computers of the 1960s were primitive when compared to those of today did little to harm the popularity of Spacewar. Computer buffs spread the knowledge of the game from one college campus to another. They spent countless hours—and millions of dollars in computer time—simulating dogfights between spaceships across a screen meant to represnt outer space.

One student who learned to play Spacewar at college was Nolan Bushnell. He was majoring in electrical engineering at the University of Utah at the time. Bushnell was later to take the concept upon which Spacewar was based and develop the world's first coin-operated video game.

As a boy growing up in Clearfield, Utah, Nolan had been a tinkerer. His favorite toys were erector sets, ham radios, and oscilloscopes, devices that

Nolan Bushnell spearheaded the development of coin-operated video games. (Pizza Time Theatre, Inc.)

used televisionlike screens to depict changes in electric current and voltage.

At college, Nolan came under the influence of Dr. David Evans, one of the pioneers in the field of computer graphics. He recalled how he and some of his classmates would go over to the computer-science department at night and play Spacewar. "It was a good game," Bushnell told *Video Games* magazine, "although a little advanced for its time."

During summer vacations, Bushnell worked as games manager at the Lagoon Amusement Park in Salt Lake City. But the games were old-fashioned. Weight-guessing was one such game. Another involved tossing baseballs at milk bottles.

Bushnell toyed with the idea of developing a new midway game—a computer game—like Spacewar. But the economics of video games didn't make sense at the time. The computer on which Bushnell and his classmates played Spacewar had cost about $8 million. At 25 cents a play, it would take two hundred years or so to accumulate enough money. Bushnell filed the idea away.

When he left college, Bushnell hoped to go to work in the research department at Disneyland. But Walt Disney wasn't interested in hiring newly graduated engineers. Bushnell moved to California permanently, to

Redwood City, and landed a job with the Ampex Corporation as a research engineer.

The computer field was growing by leaps and bounds. The integrated circuit had become a reality. Computer components were getting smaller and smaller, and cheaper and cheaper. The idea that Bushnell once had for a coin-operated video game now seemed practical.

Bushnell was married now. He and his wife and two daughters lived in a tract house in Santa Clara in the heart of Silicon Valley. After a day of work at the lab at Ampex, Bushnell would rush home, eat a fast dinner, and then shut himself away in the workshop he had put together in one of his daughter's bedrooms, whereupon she shared a room with her sister.

Bushnell would work long into the night, poring over technical diagrams and elaborately wired mazes that resembled piles of spaghetti. For a video screen, he used a raster monitor from a 19-inch black-and-white General Electric television set. His invention employed 185 integrated circuits.

Bushnell's hard work produced Computer Space, the first commercial video game, the grandfather of all arcade games. It pitted rocket ships against flying saucers, with the player controlling turn, fire, and thrust buttons. It cost 25 cents to play.

When Bushnell showed Computer Space to his engineering friends, they thought it was excellent. Bushnell then worked out an agreement with Nutting Associates, a small manufacturer of arcade games, to market Computer Space. But the game was a flop. Only about 1,500 were sold. It was simply too much of a puzzle for the average person. Bushnell realized it was ahead of its time.

Bushnell had no intention of giving up, however. He had earned about $500 in royalties from Computer Space. He used that money in 1972 to form his own company to develop video games. He called it Atari, a term he took from the Oriental game of Go and which means, approximately, "Prepare to be attacked!"

Atari was incorporated on June 27, 1972. More than a month before, Magnavox had begun introducing the Odyssey television system to dealers, distributors, sales personnel, and other interested persons by means of shows the company sponsored in various parts of the country. Late in May that year, one such show was offered in Burlingame, California, not far from San Francisco.

Bushnell attended the demonstration (as court records would later document). There he saw a simulated version of the game of Ping Pong being played. Bushnell tried out the game.

Early in the summer of 1972, Bushnell hired Allen Alcorn, a bright young computer engineer he had met at Ampex. Alcorn's first assignment was to develop a coin-operated Ping Pong game. Bushnell described what he had in mind and Alcorn executed his ideas electronically. It took him about three months, or until the fall of 1972. The game had 73 integrated circuits, each of which cost about 50 cents. They called it Pong.

Each of Pong's two players was represented by a white rectangle, which could be moved vertically. These rectangles were the players' paddles, used to bat another symbol representing the ball across a heavy broken line—the net—at the center of the screen. Big numbers reporting the score appeared at the top of the screen.

Bushnell decided to test-market the game at Andy Capp's Tavern in nearby Sunnyvale, California, to see whether anyone would play it. A couple of days after it had been installed, the owner of the tavern called Bushnell to complain that the game had broken down. Bushnell hurried over. When he opened the cabinet, he immediately saw what was wrong. The sawed-off plastic milk jug that was meant to catch the quarters was filled to overflowing. Pong was choking in money.

By 1974 tens of thousands of Pongs were in operation. Bushnell marketed the games through the traditional distributors of pinball machines and under the usual terms. The distributor leased the games to owners of arcades, candy stores, pizza parlors, and the like for one-half of each machine's revenues. It was up to the distributor to keep the machine in working order, emptying out the coin box once a week and dividing the quarters with the location's owner.

With the introduction of Pong, pinball machines began going the way of the hula hoop and Davy Crockett. Their complex electromechanical

Pong, the first successful coin-operated game, was first tried in this Sunnyvale, California, tavern formerly named *Andy Capp*'s, now called the *Country Store*. (George Sullivan)

By today's standards, Pong's video display was primitive. Large numbers at the top of the screen reported game scores.

controls required constant maintenance. But video games, with their solid-state components, could go for long periods without repairs. They were the answer to an arcade owner's prayer.

Despite Pong's enormous success, there were problems for Bushnell and Atari. Although there were some 100,000 Pongs collecting quarters around the country, they were not all Atari Pongs. Far from it. The vast majority were counterfeit machines, produced by thirty to forty other manufacturers. Game counterfeiting is a problem that continues to dog the video-game industry.

Atari moved into the home video-game field in 1975. Bushnell's engineers produced a version of Pong that could be played on standard television sets. Since Atari had no experience in consumer marketing, the company called upon Sears to sell the game. Many millions of home Pongs were sold in the next few years.

Meanwhile, Bushnell, now often hailed as King Pong by the press, was hiring engineers and designers to develop new arcade games. Pong was followed by Space Race, Pong Doubles, and Gotcha, the first video maze game. Then came two more Pong variations, Super Pong and Quadrapong. Tank, introduced late in 1974, was also a good seller.

What started with Pong was followed with Breakout, which made its debut in 1976, and Super Breakout, introduced later. Breakout was an overnight sensation. Instead of a ball being batted back and forth across a net, the idea in Breakout was to keep the ball in play for as long as possible, while knocking out multicolored bricks in a series of brick walls. The first few bricks were easy to destroy, but the closer you came to "breaking out," the more difficult the game became. The objective was the same in Super Breakout, but the graphics were better.

Some observers said that Breakout was the first "real" video game. All previous games were like Pong—that is, they were simply imitations of games already known. But Breakout could never have existed were it not for the video screen and its related electronics.

Breakout was designed by a young man once described as a "sharp kid from Palo Alto." His name was Steven Jobs. The story is that Nolan Bushnell would describe a game to Jobs and instruct him to use a specific number of integrated circuits in designing it. For each integrated circuit that Jobs was able to eliminate in the final design, he received a $100 bonus. In the case of Breakout, Jobs is said to have earned about $5,000 in bonus money.

Breakout, however, is not what gave Steven Jobs fame. He left Atari, and along with a computer wizard named Stephen Wozniak, began building a computer in the garage of his parents' home. They had started working in a bedroom, but Jobs's parents did not permit it.

The computer Jobs and Wozniak designed was inexpensive and meant for home use. Other personal computers had been developed, but Jobs's was popular because it hooked up to home television sets. Jobs and Wozniak hired additional people to produce and market their computer. When no one else could think of a name for the company, Jobs dubbed it Apple Computer. By 1980 Jobs and Apple were being looked upon as one of Silicon Valley's great success stories.

The mid-1970s was a period of drastic change in the video-game industry. Economical microprocessor chips had become a reality. The breakthrough

---

Breakout, and Super Breakout (shown here), are Pong's cousins. (Atari, Inc.)

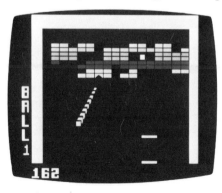

had its greatest impact on the home-game market. With chips, it became possible to develop consoles that worked on the same principal as tape recorders. To change the game, one merely inserted a different cartridge.

Fairchild Instrument and Camera Corporation was the first company to offer a programmable home-game system. RCA and Bally followed. As these systems became available to the public, the Pong home game nose-dived in popularity. After all, it was as nonprogrammable as a game of Monopoly. With Pong, all you could ever do was play Pong.

Bushnell realized Atari's need for a programmable system. By 1975 an early model of such a system had been built under the direction of Steve Mayer, who was to become an important figure in research and development for the company. The key to the system was a microprocessor chip, which Mayer nicknamed Stella. The chip made the software do as much work as possible. The hardware, relatively simple in design, could thus be cheaply produced. It was called the Video Computer System, or VCS, for short.

When seeking to mass-produce the VCS, Atari ran into several problems. The design of the system called for the use of two different metal screws so similar in size that assembly-line workers had difficulty telling them apart. When one of the larger screws was used in one of the smaller holes, it drilled out metal filings that rattled around inside the plastic case. These created chaos amid the electronic circuitry.

The plastic cases themselves were another source of trouble. When stored for a long time, the plastic sometimes warped. Then the two halves

Atari's Video Computer System as it appears today. (Atari, Inc.)

would not fit together. Workers learned to execute what they called the "VCS karate chop" to get the two halves joined.

Atari overcame these and other problems in time to get the VCS on the market for the 1977 Christmas season. But there was no great demand for it. The year 1978 was also a poor one for Atari and the VCS. All the while, Atari kept producing cartridges for the system. Once the public became aware of all the software available, sales of the VCS began picking up. Then came Space Invaders, the first video-game smash hit. Atari licensed Space Invaders for VCS use. VCS sales exploded. *Spectrum,* a magazine published by and for the Institute of Electrical and Electronics Engineers, ranked the VCS as "one of the most successful microprocessor based products ever built." Between 12 and 15 million units have been sold.

Its versatility is one reason for the VCS's success. It can play Pinball and Chess, Football and Slot Racers, and Air-Sea Battle and Codebreaker. It can also play Pac-Man and other arcade games. More than 200 different cartridges, manufactured by dozens of different companies, are available for it. The VCS, *Spectrum* declared, created an industry.

A top-selling cartridge can produce tidy profits. Each cartridge consists of the plastic cartridge itself, a few small springs to anchor the chip that carries the game program, and a small amount of additional circuitry. The total cost to the manufacturer is usually less than $5.

About as expensive as producing the cartridges, perhaps even more expensive, is the amount of money that goes into promoting them. ActiVision and Imagic, along with the other software manufacturers, buy television commercial time in large volumes.

Because of large profits and increased demand, Atari went through a period of startling growth. In the mid-1970s it was a company with fewer than a thousand employees. By the early 1980s Atari ranked as the giant of the home-entertainment game field. Its more than ten thousand employees worked in some fifty buildings strewn about California's Silicon Valley in such communities as Sunnyvale, San Jose, Santa Clara, and Milpitas. In addition, Atari operated manufacturing and assembling facilities in El Paso, Texas, and in Ireland and Taiwan. The company's annual sales kept doubling and redoubling, soaring to over a billion dollars a year.

Nolan Bushnell, however, did not preside over Atari during the period of its largest growth. He had sold the company to Warner Communications in 1976 for $528 million. According to the terms of his agreement with Warner, Bushnell was to stay on as Atari's chairman of the board, but it didn't work out that way. King Pong was dethroned in 1978.

In 1981 Atari was struck a heavy blow when several of its most valued

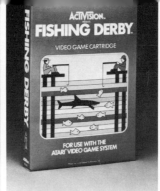

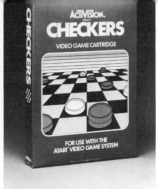

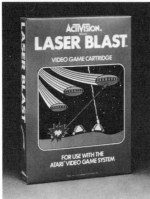

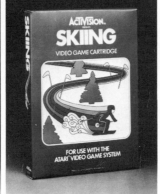

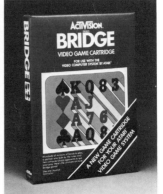

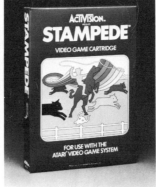

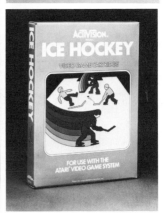

Activision cartridges designed for the Atari game system. (Activision, Inc.)

program designers and programmers left the company to form two software companies, Imagic and ActiVision. They immediately began designing games that were compatible with the Atari VCS and Intellivision, and also various home computers.

Before he left Atari, Bushnell completed one final transaction with Warner Communications. For $500,000, he bought Pizza Time Theatre, a company founded in 1974. Each Pizza Time Theatre was part pizza parlor and part video-game arcade, with a handful of performing animal robots thrown in. Bushnell described the theaters as family entertainment centers. "I think one of the real values of video games," he said, "is that they allow parents to compete with their children. I wanted a family place where parents were encouraged to do that."

By the end of 1982 there were two hundred Pizza Time Theatres in operation. Bushnell predicted there would be more than a thousand of them by the end of the decade. He said that the enterprise's mascot, a mechanical rodent named Chuck E. Cheese, was destined to become more famous than Mickey Mouse.

Bushnell divided his time between the Pizza Time Theater headquarters in Sunnyvale, California, and the offices of Catalyst Technologies, another company he founded, also in Sunnyvale. Catalyst Technologies was an umbrella corporation that provided financial support and business expertise to design engineers and others seeking to establish themselves in the high-tech field. Catalyst Technologies included such firms as Androbot (involved in the development of home robots), Vistar (educational television), Timber Tech (computer camps for kids), and Videa (video games.)

In mid-1983, it was announced that Bushnell had entered into an agreement with Atari, giving the company the rights to coin-operated video games developed by himself, Pizza-Time Theaters, and Sente Technologies, Inc., another of his companies.

Nolan Bushnell has played a key role in the history of video games. It's likely that his influence will continue.

Bushnell poses with Chuck E. Cheese, mascot for Pizza Time Theatre. (Pizza Time Theatre, Inc.)

5. The First Big Hits

In the first years that Atari's Video Computer System was available, the public pretty much ignored it. In 1978, for example, Atari built 800,000 VCS units. Only about half that number were sold, a fact that disturbed Atari executives. Other home games were not selling any better. As for arcade games of the time, no one had to line up to play them either.

At the same time, spawned by American technological developments and readily available game chips, the huge and powerful Japanese electronics industry had begun manufacturing video games. Taito was the name of the company that developed Space Invaders. In 1978, Taito sales people told representatives of the Midway Manufacturing Company in Franklin Park, Illinois, that Space Invaders was causing all kinds of excitement in Japan. Midway entered into an agreement with Taito to manufacture and distribute the game in the United States. Space Invaders triggered the first bout of video-game madness in this country.

Space Invaders seemed to be a simple game. From your laser base, you sought to destroy fifty-five alien invaders which were grouped in eleven columns, five invaders to a column. It was essentially a shoot-and-run game. You darted out from behind a shelter to zap an invader or two, then scooted back. You controlled the movement of your laser base with buttons. The game had a seductive quality to it. You always seemed on the brink of mastering it—but few people ever did.

The fact that the invaders moved faster and faster as the game progressed, one of its most enticing features, came about almost by accident. As Bill Adams, director of game development for Midway, explained: "The hardware had a limitation—it could only move a certain number of objects

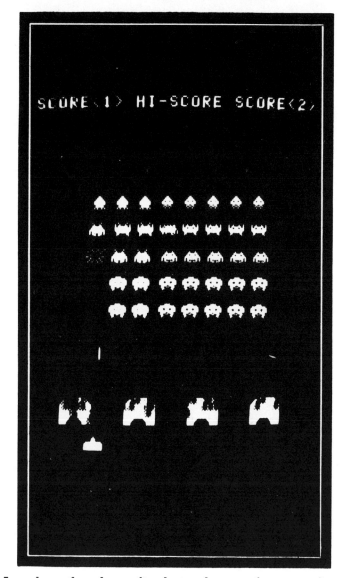

In Space Invaders, the player fired at columns of enemy aliens from the laser base near the screen's bottom edge. (Taito America Corp. Space Invaders is a trademark of Taito America Corp.)

efficiently. Once some of the invaders got shot, the hardware did not have as many objects to move, and the invaders that remained sped up."

Japan went mad over Space Invaders first. Instead of a quarter, Japanese machines used 100-yen coins. Space Invaders became so popular that a shortage of 100-yen pieces developed. The Bank of Japan had to triple production of 100-yen coins to compensate for all of those sitting in machines.

Space Invaders looked like this in the early 1980's. (George Sullivan. Space Invaders is a trademark of Taito America Corp.)

Space Invaders was the first big video-game hit in the United States. More than 55,000 machines were sold to arcade owners in 1979. Some 350,000 machines were sold worldwide. At one point in 1979, according to Steve Bloom, author of *Video Games,* more than 4 billion quarters had been pumped into the game, which added up to about one per earthling.

Space Invaders was also important from the standpoint of electronics. It was the first widely distributed arcade game to be controlled by a microchip. It would have been virtually impossible to create Space Invaders with the technology that existed previously.

Space Invaders made for some grim days at Atari's arcade division. Company executives saw the marketplace being overrun by the Japanese machine. Atari sought to answer back with such games as Starship and Super Breakout, but they did little to solve the problem.

Lyle Rains, an Atari veteran, and later vice-president of engineering, thought a game called Cosmos might make the public forget Space Invaders. Cosmos was being developed in one of the Atari Labs. It was a two-player space game involving planets and asteroids. But the asteroids couldn't move.

One day while Rains was thinking about Cosmos, he got the idea of making the asteroids move around. Ed Logg, an Atari programmer, developed a working model of such a game. The game was called Asteroids. It got to be so popular at Atari that people would drop by Ed Logg's lab just to say hello, then refuse to leave until they could try the game.

At every stage of development, Asteroids was a sensation. When the game went into production, assembly-line workers would run over and play the machines on their breaks before they were boxed and shipped. The public liked Asteroids just as much. During 1980 Atari executives started wearing smiles as Asteroids began to overshadow Space Invaders in America, selling over 70,000 games. But Asteroids was never quite the equal of Space Invaders on a worldwide basis.

In Asteroids, you, the player, controlled a triangular spaceship that dodged big rocks or blasted them. In the latter case, the rocks would be shattered into smaller rocks that also had to be dodged or destroyed. Occasionally, an enemy spaceship would come upon the scene. You got extra points for gunning it down.

During the period that Asteroids was being developed in the Atari labs, the designers and engineers sometimes racked up scores of around 90,-000. But after the game had been in national distribution for a few months, rumors began to trickle back to Atari that players were scoring well up into the millions—that they were, in fact, beating the game. Players had found a flaw in Asteroids. They had found a way to outsmart the game's program.

One of the challenges in Asteroids involved the smaller of two flying saucers that came rocketing across the screen toward the end of each asteroid attack. Players learned that if they picked off all the asteroids, except for one small and one medium asteroid, they could lie in ambush near one of the edges of the screen and wait for the saucer to appear, then blast it out of the sky for a big bonus. They could keep doing this over and over—until they accidentally destroyed one of the asteroids (triggering the start of a new attack), crashed into the saucer, or simply decided to abandon the game out of boredom or fatigue.

Daily newspapers were filled with stories of kids who had played Asteroids for thirteen or fourteen hours at a stretch and run up scores of 20 million or more. Arcade owners were very unhappy with this turn of events. As knowledge of the flaw became widespread, Asteroids machines were played more and more but took in fewer and fewer quarters. Atari retaliated by devising a microchip that erased the flaw, and provided it to arcade operators. It's tough to beat the engineers.

Designers continued to have fears that their games would contain a flaw similar to the one found in the early Asteroids machines. To allow players to tie up games for hours without really "playing" is an unpardonable sin.

After Asteroids, Atari brought out Battlezone, a three-microprocessor game. (Asteroids had two microprocessors.) Battlezone offered you, the player, the experience of driving a tank. You patrolled a battlefield that appeared on an electronic map, seeking to destroy enemy vehicles before they destroyed you. Distant objects appeared faintly at first, then brightened as they got closer, giving the appearance of three dimensions.

When the U.S. Army learned about Battlezone, they asked Atari to adapt the game so it could be used for gunnery instruction. The Army version had realistic silhouettes of both enemy and friendly tanks, other armored vehicles, and helicopters. The trainee playing the game had 10 to 25 seconds to pick the right weapon for the target, select the right ammunition, estimate the range, and destroy the target before he himself got destroyed.

Up until the latter part of 1980 virtually every successful video game featured enemy aliens or evil robots. These were games based on war, shooting, and battles in outer space. Aside from Space Invaders, Asteroids, and Battlezone, already mentioned, there were also Galaxian, Missile Command, Astro Fighter, and Defender. With this kind of history, no one was prepared for the tremendous success achieved by a game based upon a yellow dot that ran breakneck through a maze, trying to avoid pursuing monsters. The game, of course, was Pac-Man.

Pac-Man's origins were Asian. It was developed by Namco, a Japanese manufacturer. The name of its inventor was Toro Iwatani. It is said to have been derived from a Japanese nursery rhyme that told the story of a monster who devoured things very fast. "Puck-Puck-Puck" was the sound the monster made when gobbling down things.

"Puck-Man" was what the game was called in Japan. When Namco got in touch with Midway about licensing the game in the United States, the word "puck" presented a problem. It was thought to be too close to an often-heard American expletive, so "puck" was changed to "pac."

Pac-Man made its debut in the United States in November 1980 at a trade show in Chicago sponsored by the Amusement and Music Operators Association. Nobody paid too much attention to the game. It was thought to be too cute to be successful.

But when Midway began installing the game in arcades, it was an entirely different story. Young people everywhere lined up to play. They screamed in anguish and delight as they led the gobbling Pac-Man through the game's labyrinth. There was nothing complicated about the game. The player, moving a joystick, sought to negotiate a network of interconnecting pathways without being caught by four fuzzy monsters,

Pac-Man and Ms. Pac-Man also became available in tabletop editions.

(Coleco Industries, Inc. Pac-Man, trademark and © 1980, Bally-Midway Mfg. Co.)

named Speedy (nicknamed Pinky), Shadow (Blinky), Bashful (Inky), and Pokey (Clyde).

The maze passageways were lined with 240 small yellow dots. There were larger dots, called energizers, in each corner of the maze. When Pac-Man ate an energizer—also called a power pill—the monsters turned dark blue in color and could, for a few seconds, be eaten by Pac-Man. The game had bright colors and amusing sound effects.

Pac-Man enjoyed its first burst of success early in 1981. It ranked as the nation's number-one game on *Play Meter* magazine's video-game popularity chart from January to June that year, and it held on to the number-two position through the rest of the summer. An important reason for Pac-Man's popularity, arcade operators noted, was that the game appealed to girls as well as boys. That had never happened before.

Pac-Man's success could also be measured by the number of quarters it consumed. Most video games swallowed about $150 in quarters each week. But Pac-Man averaged between $200 and $240. A few locations reported as much as $800 a week per machine.

At the same time, Pac-Man proved to be a merchandizing bonanza. There were Pac-Man figurines, and you could dance to the record of "Pac-Man Fever," tie your shoes with Pac-Man laces, and wear Pac-Man pajamas, T-shirts, and caps. You could sleep in a Pac-Man sleeping bag while resting your head on a Pac-Man pillow. There were Pac-Man bumper stickers—"I Brake for Pac-Man"—bed trays, and lapel pins. There were Pac-Man paper plates, cups, napkins, and table cloths. You could paper your room with Pac-Man wallpaper and hang Pac-Man drapes. Popsicle Products introduced a Pac-Man ice pop. The Calfex Company manufactured a Pac-Man doll. When you talked to it, it replied with the familiar

Coleco marketed a series of Pac-Man collectible figures. (Coleco Industries, Inc. Pac-Man, trademark and © 1980, Bally-Midway Mfg. Co.)

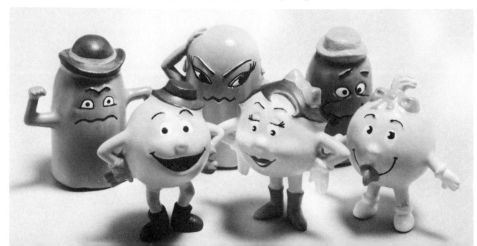

Ms. Pac-Man came to rival Pac-Man in popularity. (George Sullivan. Ms. Pac-Man, trademark and © 1981 Bally-Midway Mfg. Co.)

wukka-wukka-wukka sound the game made. The more you talked, the more *it* talked.

Well over one hundred manufacturers eventually jumped on the Pac-Man bandwagon, offering over five hundred different products. Pac-Man came to rank right up there with Snoopy and Miss Piggy.

As a result of all of this activity, Pac-Man shot back up in popularity as an arcade game. And Pac-Man got still another boost in 1982 as cartridges for home use began to appear. Advertisements reading "Guess Who's Coming to Dinner," and "We Can't Go on Eating Like This" appeared in daily newspapers and magazines to announce Atari's game cartridge. Coleco brought out a table-top edition of the game, which was also heavily advertised.

Atari named April 3, 1982, as Pac-Man Day. A larger-than-life costumed version of Pac-Man and the monster Speedy toured a number of cities by means of special Pac-Vans. The pair visited hospitals and appeared at shopping malls and major sports events. For the first time, a video-game character threw out the first ball at a baseball game.

Midway was quick to follow-up on Pac-Man's success. In January 1982 the company introduced a game called Ms. Pac-Man. The leading character was a yellow disk with ruby lips, fluttering eyelashes, and a little bow in her hair. Before the end of the year Ms. Pac-Man had climbed to the top of the *Play Meter* chart.

After Ms. Pac-Man, Midway released Super Pac-Man, Baby Pac-Man, and Pac-Man Plus. It's likely that the gobbler characters, in one way or another, will occupy game arcades and America's living rooms for many years to come.

Space Invaders served to introduce millions of Americans to video games. Asteroids demonstrated that games were no temporary craze. Pac-Man broadened their popularity, establishing video games as an important leisure-time activity. These three games had scores and scores of imitators during the 1980s. Following Space Invaders—basically a shoot-and-run game—came Astro Blaster, Galaxian, Centipede, and Phoenix.

Asteroids led to a flood of outer-space games. They included Space Fury, Space Odyssey, Star Castle, Space Duel, and Defender. Of these, Defender deserves special mention. Your mission in the game was to defend a humanoid population from several types of flying aliens, each with a different shape, color, and character. When the aliens had kidnapped all of the humans, you found yourself surrounded by violent mutants and your end was near.

The control system in Defender was unusual. It involved a two-directional joystick, a fire button (to move your ship through space), a smart-bomb button (which wiped out all the aliens on the screen at one time), and a hyperspace button (which caused your ship to rematerialize in some random location on the screen). While some players were bewildered by all of this and never attempted to play the game, Defender had a large and loyal group of supporters.

In Pac-Man's wake came dozens of maze games such as Berzerk, Frog-

Defender's control panel could bewilder a beginner. (George Sullivan)

Donkey Kong eventually replaced Pac-Man as the nation's favorite game.
(Aime LaMontagne. Donkey Kong is a trademark of Nintendo America, Inc.)

ger, Turtles, Lock 'n' Chase, Centipede, Make Traks, Burger Time, Tutankham, and Pengo. Reflex action games also became popular. In these, you were usually cast in the role of the driver of a racing car, as in Monaco GP, Turbo, or Pole Position. You could also be the pilot of a supersonic fighter plane as it zoomed through the sky. Scramble and Zaxxon were the most noted games of that type.

One other game became extremely popular during this period. It didn't fit into any of the usual categories. In this game you played the part of a determined little carpenter named Mario who sought to rescue a beautiful woman held captive by a bad-tempered gorilla. You had to ascend the skeleton of an unfinished skyscraper to get to the woman, while the ape threw barrels down at you. Sound familiar? It was Donkey Kong, the game that supplanted Pac-Man as America's number-one video hit.

It used to be said that video games were a fad, that their popularity was only temporary, that the public would soon tire of them for something else. Space Invaders was a fad. So was Asteroids. Pac-Man was faddish, too. But as quickly as one of these games began to diminish in popularity, another took its place in the public's esteem. Individual games may induce temporary crazes but video games collectively are here to stay.

6. Designing the Games—I

At the age of twenty-four, Rob Fulop, a game designer for Imagic, earned close to $100,000 a year, drove an expensive BMW, and owned a townhouse not far from San Francisco. *Newsweek* magazine called him a young wizard. Rob Fulop was one of a growing army of video-game designers. They worked for Atari, creating games for both arcade and home use; for Mattel and Coleco; and for such software specialists as Imagic, Activision, Parker Brothers, and others.

Fulop was the designer who created Demon Attack, one of the big home-video game hits of recent times. *Electronic Games* magazine named it "Video Game of the Year" in 1982. In Demon Attack you were required to do battle against an array of brilliantly colored and increasingly menacing birdlike creatures. Imagic produced different editions of the game for the Atari VCS, Intellivision, and a number of other hardware systems. Fulop said that it was the "appeal of the unexpected" that helped to make Demon Attack so successful. Each wave of demons looked entirely different. Kids kept playing it so they could see all the exciting transformations.

Fulop got into game designing by accident. He was what he called an "average" student at the University of California at Berkeley. He majored in computer sciences. Not long before he graduated, he saw a notice on the bulletin board at the university career center about a job at Atari. "Most of my friends wanted to go to work for IBM or companies like that," Fulop recalled. "Few of them had ever heard of Atari."

He was hired by Atari a few months after he graduated. Not long after, Fulop created Night Driver, a scarily realistic game in which the player was the driver of a speeding car on a pitch-black night. Cars approached from the opposite direction, their headlights flashing, their horns blaring. The

Rob Fulop (*left*) and two of his colleagues at Imagic, Dave Johnson (*center*) and Bruce Pedersen. (Imagic, Inc.)

road kept twisting and turning. Night Driver became one of Atari's most successful games.

Fulop scored another success when he adapted the popular Missile Command, which existed only as an arcade game at the time, for use with the Atari's VCS. He left Atari in 1981 to join Imagic. "Video games should be simple," Fulop said. "You shouldn't need an instruction book to learn how to play a game. You should be able to pick it up right away. But a game should also be complex. It should reveal itself to you over a period of several weeks; otherwise, you'll get tired of it."

Designing a video game is something like writing a novel. It begins as an idea in someone's mind. A certain setting is established—outer space, a mushroom patch, or an abandoned uranium mine. A main character is invented, then put into certain situations. A story evolves that is filled with action and adventure. It cannot lag for a second. As the scenario gets longer and more involved, parts of the original idea may be dropped and subplots may be added. A great deal of time is spent revising.

Where do game ideas come from? "They can come from anywhere," said Don Osborne, vice-president of sales and marketing at Atari. "A good idea is like a seed," he added. "Hopefully, it is something that is going to sprout.

"We usually don't consider ideas that come to us from outside sources," said Osborne. "If I was to receive material describing a game, I'd fire it right down to the legal department. The legal people usually return it to the sender, explaining we do not accept unsolicited material.

"It's not that we're not interested," Osborne said. "It's just that the real

About thirty designers work at Activision. Senior designers include: (*left to right*) Larry Kaplan, Alan Miller, David Crane, Steve Cartwright, and Bob Whitehead. (Activision, Inc.)

'secret' in the success of a game is not the basic idea. It's the game-play action that eventually gets put into it. That's the quality that keeps the player coming back to the game time and time again.''

Anyone who works for Atari can submit an idea. "We get contributions from engineers and salesmen, and about half of the company's secretaries have submitted ideas," Osborne said. They describe the game's basic concept and explain how it is to be played. Some people even have storyboards prepared. These are drawings that depict the game as it progresses from one level to the next.

People who have submitted ideas are then organized into groups of as many as fifteen or twenty people. They get together at someone's house and discuss the ideas one by one, refining each. The best of the ideas are given to artists or graphic designers, and fuller treatments of them are prepared.

All of the ideas—there may be as many as two hundred of them—are then presented at an annual planning session that lasts several days, and that is attended by representatives of the engineering, design, research, marketing, and sales departments. Each game concept is evaluated from several different points of view. The marketing prospects for each game are cited and the engineers specify the technology each might demand.

"We try to make these planning sessions as informal as possible," Osborne said. "They're held, not in the office, but in a resort setting—at Pebble Beach, for instance—away from the telephone and other office distractions. Everyone dresses casually. Sweatshirts and jeans are common. We want everyone to be relaxed."

From out of the planning session comes a thick manual describing the best games. The manual, which may contain as many as a hundred game descriptions, is the source from which company designers draw when seeking ideas for new games.

After a game is assigned to a designer, he or she begins writing the game program. While most designers do their own programming, and the terms *designer* and *programmer* are frequently used interchangeably, more and more distinction has evolved between the two professions. In Japan, where scores of games that have been successful in this country have been developed, there is a definite difference. After a Japanese designer has prepared an elaborate account of the game with small drawings depicting the action in a frame-by-frame sequence, the description is turned over to a programmer. The programmer then writes the instructions telling the hardware what to do.

The distinction between designing and programming has also been found at Broderbund Software, one of the leading American companies in the development of games for computers. Some observers say that the pattern at Broderbund of separation and distinction between designers and programmers will emerge at other companies, too.

If you happen to be computer literate, you know that BASIC is the language most often used by newcomers to programming. (The programs that appear on pages 52 and 53 are written in BASIC.) BASIC is an acronym that stands for *Beginners All-Purpose Symbolic Instruction Code*. BASIC is easy to use in small computers, but it is not suitable for writing video games. Animating many multicolored objects across a screen at high speeds requires thousands of calculations per second. If this were attempted in BASIC, there would be delays in the movements of the objects; they would move jerkily.

Professional video-game programmers program in assembly, a program language similar to the English language that breaks BASIC down into digital codes. In other words, it is closer to the computer's internal binary language. Assembly programs assure movement that is smooth and fluid.

There are, of course, several other qualities a designer must have besides skill in the use of assembly. He or she also has to be highly imaginative. "I remember when I was in college," said Dona Bailey, a designer at Videa, "and hearing the term 'functional fixedness.' It means looking at an object such as a hammer and not being able to think of it as being used for anything else but hammering. A designer can't be tied down by functional fixedness. He or she has to be able to look at objects in an offbeat way."

"You also have to have an appreciation of game play," said Pat Ransil,

A Game Program

If you have access to a small computer at home, school, or a local branch of the public library, you can program it to display an elementary version of Ping Pong. The program presented on these pages, written in BASIC adapted for each of several different home computers, will enable you to bounce a ball around within an enclosed area that is framed by the screen edges. While the "game" won't do a great deal to entertain you, it serves as an introduction to programming techniques. It will also enable you to learn some of the sound and graphics capabilities of the computer.

Program for Apple Computers

```
100 GR : REM LO-RES GRAPHICS
110 GOSUB 1000: REM DRAW BORDER
120 X = 20:Y = 20
130 XVECTR = 1:YVECTR = - 1: REM START WITH
    UPPER DIAGONAL RIGHT DIRECTION
140 PT = SCRN( X + XVECTR,Y + YVECTR): REM
    LOOK AT POINT
150 IFPT=15 THEN XVECTR=-XVECTR:YVECTR=-YVE
    CTR:REM IF WALL HIT,REVERSE DIRECTION
160 COLOR= 0: PLOT X,Y: REM ERASE OLD BALL
170 X = X + XVECTR:Y = Y + YVECTR: REM
    UPDATE X,Y
180 COLOR= 1: PLOT X,Y
190 GOTO 140
999 END
1000 COLOR= 15
1010 FOR I = 0 TO 39: PLOT I,0: NEXT : REM
     YOU COULD USE HLIN 0,39 AT 0
1020 FOR I = 0 TO 39: PLOT I,39: NEXT
1030 FOR I = 0 TO 39: PLOT 0,I: NEXT
1040 FOR I = 0 TO 39: PLOT 39,I: NEXT
1050 RETURN
```

Program for PET, Atari, VIC 20, and VIC 64

```
100 SCR=PEEK(88)+256*PEEK(89):REM ADDRESS OF
    SCREEN MEMORY
105 REM USE SCR=32768 FOR PET/CBM,SCR=7680
    FOR 5K VIC
110 WALL=128:REM WALL CHARACTER, SOLID
    SQUARE.TRY OTHER CHARACTERS.
115 REM WALL=160 FOR PET/CBM/VIC
120 LN=40:REM LENGTH OF A LINE. USE LN=22
    FOR VIC,LN=80 FOR CBM 8032
130 GOSUB 260:REM DRAW BORDER
140 LOC=SCR+LN*10+LN/2:REM LOCATION OF BALL
    ON SCREEN AT FIRST
150 VECTR=LN:REM ALSO TRY -1,+1,LN-1,LN+1,
    ETC.
160 BLANK=0:REM BLANK=32 FOR PET/CBM/VIC
170 FIGURE=84:REM "BALL" CHARACTER. USE
    FIGURE =81 FOR PET/CBM/VIC
180 IF PEEK(LOC+VECTR)<>WALL THEN 200
190 VECTR=-VECTR:REM REVERSE DIRECTION
200 POKE LOC,BLANK:REM ERASE OLD BALL
210 LOC=LOC+VECTR:REM CALCULATE NEW POSITION
220 POKE LOC,FIGURE:REM PLACE BALL
230 GOTO 180
240 END
250 REM BORDER SUBROUTINE
260 PRINT CHR$(125);:REM CLEAR SCREEN. USE
    PRINT CHR$(147) FOR PET/CBM/VIC
270 FOR I=0 TO LN-1:POKE SCR+I,WALL:NEXT I:
    REM TOP
280 FOR I=0 TO LN-1:POKE SCR+LN*22+I,WALL:
    NEXT I:REM BOTTOM
290 FOR I=0 TO 22:POKE SCR+I*LN,WALL:NEXT I:
    REM LEFT
300 FOR I=0 TO 22:POKE SCR+LN-1+I*LN,WALL:
    NEXT I:REM RIGHT
310 RETURN
```

senior systems engineer at Imagic. "You have to understand what makes a game enjoyable. You have to be able to give the players the idea that if they they can attain a certain level of skill, they can control their own destinies on the screen. You can never permit a player to be wiped out haphazardly.

"The game also has to be challenging. The level of difficulty has to be pushed from one plateau to another, each requiring a greater degree of skill to master. I personally like quick-reaction games, rather than those that employ complicated strategy. In Atlantis [the Intellivision version of which Ransil designed], success depends on your ability to react fast and manipulate the controls accordingly. You have to act *now!* That's the type of game I like to write.

"A designer needs a good sense of graphics, too," Ransil said. "When I'm interviewing a designer for a job, I'll explain the graphics tools we have available, and then I'll ask the person to demonstrate his or her ability with the equipment. I'll also ask him or her to describe some game ideas, and to sketch the central figures. I just want to determine whether the person is capable of using sketches to communicate the idea.

"The ability to communicate is very important in this field," said Ransil. People are always bouncing ideas around about new games. And when you're designing a game, you're always seeking out ideas from other people. We look for people who can function in that type of environment.

"And we want our people to be highly motivated, real self-starters. Designers are given a free reign in deciding when they want to work and for how long. There's no time clock here. Imagic's main computer is in operation twenty-four hours a day, seven days a week. Each designer has his or her own terminal. If a designer wants to work a schedule from nine A.M. to five P.M., Monday through Friday, he or she can do so. But some designers prefer to start work at four o'clock in the afternoon and work through the night until breakfast. That's okay, too. No one checks to see how many pages of work you might have turned out in a given period. As a designer, you're expected to take the responsibility for the development of a particular game, and make that game as good as you can," Ransil said.

"But even though one designer is in charge of developing a game, many people contribute. For example, I may be in my office programming, and someone may walk in, watch my screen for a while, and say, 'Hey, what do you think about this?', and make a suggestion. That's how some of our best ideas result.

"Take my Atlantis game. It opens in midday, goes through the evening hours, and then nighttime comes and the sky is black. You can see the enemy only by means of searchlights. Lighting the sky in that manner was the idea of Mike Becker, one of our graphic artists. That's the way games are created. It's a team effort."

There are a number of differences between arcade games and those intended for use with home systems. Designers have to be aware of these differences. "The arcade game," said Pat Ransil, "has to be designed to play for only about ninety seconds, at least as far as the average player is concerned. At that point, the player 'loses,' and another quarter has to be inserted. There's nothing like that in the case of cartridges for games played at home. Your chief motive is to make the game enjoyable. You can make it last for hours, if you want.

"The designer also has to be aware of the pluses and minuses of the system that he or she is designing for," said Ransil. "Take Imagic's Demon Attack, for instance, which was first designed for the Atari VCS. One of the features of the VCS is that it permits smooth and easy movement across the screen in a horizontal direction. Vertical movement, on the other hand, can be troublesome. Thus, when Rob Fulop designed Demon Attack for the VCS, he programmed the demons to move mostly on a horizontal plane. But when Gary Kato designed the Intellivision version of Demon Attack, he was not so limited. He could provide Demon movement in any direction —and did."

The color of the demons provides another example of how a system's electronics can influence game design. In the Atari version of Demon

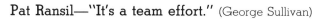

Pat Ransil—"It's a team effort." (George Sullivan)

Attack, the demons are of many different colors, because the Atari system provides for this. But Intellivision doesn't. The Intellivision demons never wear more than two colors.

Sometimes essential features of a game are stumbled upon almost by accident. Take the case of Centipede, a game recently popular in both homes and arcades. In the game, a multisegmented centipede appeared at the top of the screen and descended slowly through a field of mushrooms, row by row. You, the player, controlled a gun at the bottom of the playfield. You had to destroy the centipede segments before any one of them collided with your gun.

"Once, in the early stages of the game's development," said Dona Bailey, the game's designer, "when I was working on the path the centipede takes, I would mark the screen with a small block at every point where a centipede section was shot." As Bailey explained, a programmer needs some visual reminder of where collisions occur on the screen. Otherwise, things can get hopelessly confused.

"Well, this day I had pretty well filled up the screen with these little blocks. And someone came up behind me, watched for a while, and said, 'Hey, look at the maze game you've got there.'

" 'Maze game?' I shouted. He was right, of course, I had created a maze game with all of those little blocks, and I hadn't even realized it. We decided to leave it as a maze game, but we changed the shape of the little blocks to mushrooms. Everytime a centipede section got shot, a mushroom would be left in its place."

Once the designer has settled upon the basics, he or she begins "ramping up" the game, taking it through its various screens or boards, making each a little bit more difficult than the one previous.

The next step is to create different versions of the game. There are easy, difficult, and more difficult versions. There are one-, two-, three-, and four-player variations. There can be, in fact, dozens of different options of various kinds.

After several months of hard work, the game program runs to many thousands of lines, each densely packed with alpha-numerical characters. If there is a character out of place anywhere within those thousands of lines, the program will not work properly. Many more long, hard hours go into getting the mistakes—called "bugs"—out of the program.

Even the tiniest bug can be a problem. If a program has a flaw in it, the mistake will be repeated over and over, perhaps as many as a quarter of a million times, when the game goes into production. As Pat Ransil said, "There are no small mistakes in this business."

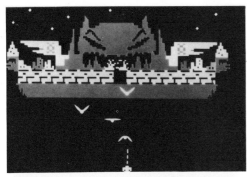

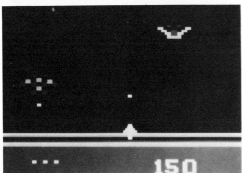

Game programs may be revised slightly to accommodate the individual features of each hardware system. The variations in Imagic's Demon Attack are shown here for *(top to bottom)* Intellivision, Odyssey², Atari VCS, and Commodore VIC-20. (Imagic, Inc.)

Dona Bailey, designer of the very popular Centipede game. (George Sullivan)

7. Designing the Games—II

Besides being a source of exciting fun, video games can be considered a twentieth-century art form of sorts. Stroll through an arcade and glance at a dozen screens. The graphics can't help but dazzle you.

There are outer-space fantasylands alive with asteroids, satellites, and weird space modules. There are animated cartoon characters populating mazes and dancing about clever geometric patterns. Other backdrops include World War II battlefields, Alpine slopes, and the desert wastes of the Sahara.

Even the names suggest graphics diversity. There are Dark Planet and Haunted House, Sea Battle and Space War, and Drag Strip and Cat 'n' Mouse. And don't overlook Frog Bog.

The festival of vivid, pulsating color keeps getting better and better. Remember Pong, the first successful coin-op game? Well, Pong had no color; it was strictly black and white. And the animation consisted of a white rectangle that bounced back and forth between two white paddles against a stark black background. It was strictly kindergarten stuff by current standards.

Games today are able to generate real visual excitement. One reason for this is that graphics artists are playing an increasingly important role in game development. While a designer may do the preliminary sketching on his or her video terminal, at many firms an artist will take these sketches and put them into final form.

To the graphic artist, the computer screen is a simple grid, a network of horizontal and vertical lines. A point on the screen is established by telling the computer, in effect, that the point is a certain amount across (an "x" value) and a certain amount up (a "y" value). Once two points have been established, the computer will draw a line between them.

The computer is also capable of handling three-dimensional objects. Let's take the example of a geometric drawing of a brick. Once the computer representation of the brick is on its tape, it can feed the drawing back onto the screen when the correct button on the keyboard is pressed. It can show the side or front views of the brick. Not only that, but the computer can also show a variety of angled views of the brick, views which give the impression of a third dimension.

The brick at this point is merely an outline drawing that looks like the framework of a brick. The computer can turn it into a solid object in a matter of seconds. It can then display a small detail of the brick or push the brick back so far it becomes a tiny dot.

The computer can be programmed to show the effect of a light shining upon the brick. The designer first encodes where the light source is to be —up close, far away, or somewhere in between—and then watches to see that the brick appears with the appropriate shadings and highlights.

The computer has color capability, too. The brick can be made to appear in any one of an infinite number of colors. In effect, the designer has an electronic brush and palette at his command.

The computer's greatest benefit to video-game designers is speed. Animated designs that once required days or even weeks of painstaking hand-crafted work can now be produced in a matter of hours.

Recently developed computer-assisted graphics equipment, by Via Video, introduced almost magical design capabilities. By pressing a device that looks like a stylus upon an electronic pad, the artist could throw any one of an infinite number of shapes—straight lines, curved lines, squares, rectangles, circles, or ellipses—onto a video screen in the blink of an eye.

A designer using a light pen with computer-assisted graphics equipment.
(George Sullivan)

He or she could also do free-hand drafting. In addition, the system provided an electronic pallet that put thousands of different colors at the artist's fingertips. Once the design was created its various elements could be moved about the screen in much the same way you might move dominoes on a table top.

Thanks to a device called a digitizer, sequence photographs, or scenes from a video tape, could also be shown upon the screen. For example, if the designer were working on the development of a football game, he or she could have sequence photos taken of a quarterback passing the ball, display them on the screen, and then adapt the sequence in preparing the game's animation. Any design or design sequence could be stored on disks and retrieved when needed.

Once the design of a game is completed, it is tried out on a breadboard. This consists of an experimental assemblage of the integrated circuits and other electronic and electric components that make up the game. At Atari, a group of employees is assigned to test new games for flaws. They play them over and over for a period of two weeks.

"These individuals used to be just assistants of one type or another, but now we call them 'video game analysts,'" said George Kiss, director of Software Development for Atari. "They can take about any game and start racking up high scores in a relatively short period of time. We use these individuals not only to test out games, but to give us a critical analysis, tell us what's good and bad about them."

At Imagic, when a game is in the final stages of development, neighborhood boys and girls between fourteen and eighteen are called upon to lend a helping hand. Said Imagic's Pat Ransil: "We invite a half a dozen or so kids to come to our offices [in Los Gatos, California] after school, and play the new games, play them over and over, trying to find any bugs they might contain. Not only do these kids have to be pretty good game players, but they also have to have the ability to explain things."

Before a game is put into production, it is thoroughly tested. Atari turns over its new games to a market research company. Like Imagic, the firm's researchers seek out game players and pay them to try out the game. On one day, the users might be males between the ages of fourteen and eighteen; on another day, they might be females from sixteen to twenty. The research has involved many such groupings.

The game is placed in a big room, one wall of which is a see-through mirror. The game's project leader, its chief designer, and other members of the development team watch through the wall to get an idea of how the

A video game designer points out a silicon chip on a circuit breadboard.
(Atari, Inc.)

players react to the game. The players know they are being watched, but they don't know how many people are watching or what they're looking for.

"When I attend these sessions, I look for emotional response on the part of the player," said Atari's Don Osborne. "I look for signs of anger and frustration. When a person pounds the control panel upon losing a man or a life, it's a strong indication that he or she is really involved in the game. Or the player may let out a loud groan, or shriek 'Oh, no!' at the top of his or her lungs. When a person doesn't show any emotional reaction on losing a life, it's a tipoff that he or she doesn't care much about the game.

"Another way to tell whether a player is really interested in a game is to simply put your hand on the side of the cabinet as the game is being played. When a player is enthusiastic about a game, you can feel the energy, the vibrations, as the joystick is moved about. Players have been known to topple over games by wrenching the joystick back and forth.

"It's a *bad* sign when a youngster sits around and sips a Coke or something, and fails to pay attention when someone else is playing the game. I like to see nonplayers act as observers, watching what's going on."

At the same time the players are being watched through the one-way mirror, they are also being monitored and questioned by the researchers. Game times—that is, how long each individual manages to play the game —are recorded. Comments are collected. Were the controls easy to master? What did he or she think of the game's graphics? Of the music and sound effects? Was the game challenging enough? Or too easy?

After a number of these sessions, the game is tested in an arcade for a period of from eight to twelve weeks. Arcade customers play the game. Afterward, each player is interviewed in depth by a researcher. In addition, a careful record is kept of the game's earnings. The game is also placed in street locations—such as pizza parlors, bus depots, and bowling centers. Again, collections are monitored.

The results of the research are carefully evaluated, and modifications may be made in the game as a result of what was learned during the research.

In the case of a game that tests successfully, the final step is to manufacture the game's microprocessors. Some games have required as many as three microprocessors. The memory modules and game control systems are also put into production.

Another group of designers plans the cabinet that will hold the game's electronics, controls, and video screen. They also create the artwork that is displayed on the control panel and cabinet sides—artwork that will reflect the game's theme.

All of this, from the first mention of the game concept at the brainstorming session, to the final packaging of the game, is done within a high degree of secrecy. The video-game industry is highly competitive and each company has an overriding fear that its rivals will learn of game concepts it has in development and plan games that are similar. Visitors are barred from design and engineering laboratories. Conversations outside of company offices and work spaces are guarded.

"This is really a small society, a closed society," said one Silicon Valley

A silk screen technician checks detail of side panel printing for an Atari game cabinet. (Atari, Inc.)

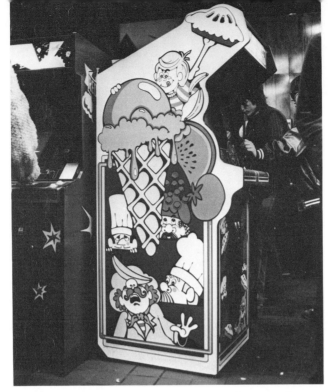

Side panel art may reflect the game's theme or feature the game's characters. This panel, for Atari's Food Fight, does both. (George Sullivan. Food Fight is a trademark of Atari, Inc.)

game designer. "You have to be careful. I'll be out playing racquetball, and the person in the next court may be from a competing company. You meet other designers at restaurants and the supermarket. So you have to be careful. We don't feel rival companies are involved in espionage activity, but we do have to protect our ideas. After all, they're the basis of our success."

In one recent year at Atari, about a dozen games went through the development process and reached the stage where they were ready for testing. But only eight of these games cleared the final hurdle, were put into production, and eventually placed in arcades. Four were dumped because it was decided they would not be successful. Today, they're gathering dust in an Atari warehouse somewhere in Silicon Valley.

Once a game is put onto the market, arcade patrons quickly form an opinion about it. They'll either line up to play it or shun it. But it's not wise to tinker with the game concept at this stage. Not only is it costly to do so, but the public does not accept changes very well. Jungle King is an example. A very successful game during the summer of 1982, Jungle King featured a hero who swung from one vine to another and emitted a Tarzan-type yell when doing so. The artwork on the cabinet side panels resembled that of the old Tarzan comic strip.

The trouble was that the resemblance was too close. The creators of the original Tarzan sued the manufacturers of Jungle King claiming copyright infringement. The company was forced to revise the games graphics, abolish the yell, and change its name to Jungle Hunt. It immediately nosedived in popularity.

Games today have to win a very broad audience. They must appeal not only to hard-core players but also to the average players—to those who look upon video games as light entertainment. Sometimes a game will be exciting and challenging but fails to appeal to a wide enough segment of the market. Gravitar, introduced in 1982, was one such game. "It was too technical, too specific," Don Osborne recalled. "It did very well on college campuses, but not in other locations.

"In order to do well in Gravitar, you first had to become skilled in playing Asteroids, Lunar Lander, and Defender. These games were kind of prerequisites. If you hadn't studied these 'subjects,' you couldn't 'take' Gravitar," Osborne said.

In the past, it sometimes took from eighteen to twenty-four months to develop an arcade game. But not anymore. The whole process has been speeded up to about six months. In the case of an original game cartridge for home use, it may take only three or four months from the time the idea is hatched until the game is put into production.

"Designing video games gives me a great deal of satisfaction," said Imagic's Pat Ransil, "much more satisfaction than I get from designing the standard computer program. Normally, when I design a program, the result is a printout. But with a video game, you get a graphic representation of the program on the screen; you get something that is pleasing to the eye.

"Then, after the game is produced in cartridge form, there can be even greater rewards. You can walk into a store where they sell game software, and they might be demonstrating a game you designed, and you see kids playing it and having fun. I like to see that. It gives you a good feeling to know that you've created something that can give enjoyment to others."

8. The War Over Video Games

Once video games became nationally popular, and teenagers and younger children began feeding quarters by the billions into the likes of Pac-Man, Defender, Centipede, and Dig-Dug, a wave of criticism broke out over the industry. The games were referred to by some people as "electronic drugs." It was said they were "addictive." They were branded as being unhealthy for children in that they retarded emotional and psychological development.

Industry critics said that game themes were based upon good-guy-versus-bad-guy confrontations. There was nothing friendly about them. Your goal was to destroy the enemy before the enemy got a chance to destroy you. It was said that such thinking could only have a damaging effect upon the young child.

In 1981 and 1982 municipalities in many parts of the country began holding special council meetings to deal with the "video madness" that had beset their communities. The board of trustees in the town of Irvington in Westchester County, New York, won nationwide attention in June 1981 when it debated prohibiting children under the age of seventeen from entering game arcades. In Pittsburgh, the City Council, concerned that children were skipping school to play video games, approved an ordinance that barred students from arcades during school hours. Any arcade that violated the law would lose its license.

The perception that video games might be potentially dangerous to the young was not limited to the United States. President Ferdinand E. Marcos of the Philippines banned video games in November 1981 after parents complained that the games were wreaking "havoc in the morality of the nation's youth." Indonesia issued a ban on games in 1982 and Malaysia considered following suit. "Video games are destroying our traditional games," said the spokesman for a Malaysian consumer group, "and our children are no longer interested in, say, flying kites or top-spinning."

New games and game arcades had been attacked before. During the 1930s, when pinball began to rise in popularity, pinball machines took over the arcades of the day, which were found chiefly at amusement parks and vacation resorts. As the popularity of pinball continued to grow, some adults declared that children were wasting their time and money. Arcades were condemned as corrupt and detrimental places. Some communities banned pinball machines. Others passed laws prohibiting children from entering arcades.

There is also a parallel between the reaction to the sudden popularity of video games and what took place not long after the turn of the century when motion pictures first began to attain widespread popularity. In New York City, on January 18, 1909, the city's Aldermanic Committee on Laws and Legislation began hearings on a proposed ordinance that would prohibit the admission of children under the age of sixteen to motion-picture shows unless accompanied by a parent or guardian. Much of the testimony, as reported in *The New York Times,* would have a familiar ring today.

Alderman Bent, who introduced the legislation, declared that many of the motion picture shows "were not run by 'fit persons.' " He also stated that the records of the children's court showed that "a great many youngsters stole in order to get money to attend the places."

Sergeant Preston of the Brooklyn Children's Society testified that his organization had found that hundreds of children who should have been in school were truant and went to the shows. He confirmed that children stole to obtain the price of admission. He also declared that many girls had been "led astray" in attending the shows. Another witness said that children were taking the money given to them for lunch and spending it for admission.

"The Reverend John Lewis Clark of Brooklyn and several others presented arguments of the same character," said the article in the *Times.* "No one appeared who was opposed to the ordinance."

During the recent controversy over video games, Mrs. Ronnie Lamm of Centereach, Long Island, gained national recognition for her efforts to regulate game arcades in her community. To some she became the "hatchet queen of amusement centers," a tag she considered absurd. "There was a problem to be addressed," Mrs. Lamm said, "and we addressed it."

The mother of Jennifer, a nine-year-old girl, and Everett, a thirteen-year-

Ronnie Lamm—"There was a problem to be addressed, and we addressed it." (George Sullivan)

old boy, Mrs. Lamm served as the president of the local PTA District Council, which involved twelve schools and some fourteen thousand students. She had a master's degree in early-childhood education and had taught first grade and also secondary school.

"We first became concerned about the video games in the fall of 1981," Mrs. Lamm said. "They started showing up everywhere—in our malls and shopping centers, in local pizza places, corner delicatessans, bakeries, and even the laundromat."

It was easy for the youngsters of the community to get to the games, either by walking or riding their bicycles. "They didn't have to be driven," Mrs. Lamm said. "They could play them about when they pleased. We began to notice that the kids were spending more and more time—and more and more quarters—on these games. We got an uncomfortable feeling about what the games were doing to our community."

Mrs. Lamm and others began a campaign to persuade the town of Brookhaven, Long Island—which includes many smaller communities such as Centereach, Selden, Coram, Middle Island, and Lake Ronkonkoma—to stop issuing game permits for a period of six months. The campaigners circulated petitions, made speeches before official bodies and community groups, sent out mailings, and talked with local and state officials.

Mrs. Lamm was successful. Early in 1982 the Town of Brookhaven declared it would issue no additional game permits for a period of six months. At the time she began her campaign, there were seventeen applications to open video-game arcades in her community. Twelve of those applications were denied, while five others were withdrawn.

But this was only the beginning. Mrs. Lamm's efforts attracted the attention of the media. She was the subject of feature articles in several video-game magazines and dozens of daily newspapers, including the *New York Times.* "Mrs. Lamm is one of a rapidly growing army," said the *Times,* "that is rising up in communities across the country to beat back the tide of Space Invaders, Asteroids, and Astro Blasters." She championed the anti-video-game cause on the "Phil Donohue Show" and other television programs. More and more, she came to be identified as the principal spokesperson for those who opposed video games.

After her initial victory, Mrs. Lamm intensified her efforts to get the community to exert even greater control over arcades and games. She now objected to the games for two more-specific reasons—for the violence they portrayed and because she felt they undermined a youngster's ability to communicate.

"They breed aggressive behavior," Mrs. Lamm said. Specifically, she objected to a game called Fire Bug. "You get points for how many floors of a building you set afire. That's frightening!" Mrs. Lamm did not even like Pac-Man. "Gobbling up cookies on a screen. What do those cookies represent?"

"Watching violence on television can cause violent behavior on the part of kids," she said. "That's been documented." She felt the same concept

---

Legislation in the Town of Brookhaven now mandates that game rooms be closed during school hours. (George Sullivan)

applied to video games. Mrs. Lamm also took issue with the games because, as she put it, "They mesmerize our kids," and because of potential physical harm. "Try talking to a kid after he or she has come out of any arcade. It's like talking to a kid who is wearing a Walkman," she said, and Mrs. Lamm believed that "rays coming out from the screen" could damage one's vision or even cause cancer.

As for the arcades, one reason Mrs. Lamm objected to them was that she believed children skipped school to play games in the arcades. "Video games are not the *cause* of kids skipping school," she stressed. "But the arcades are a warm place for the kids to hang out in the fall and winter. If the kids have a warm place to go instead of school, won't they opt for it?"

Mrs. Lamm dismissed the idea that video games improve hand-eye coordination, a claim frequently put forth by those who support the games. "As an elementary school teacher, hand-eye coordination was something I was very much concerned with. It's not a skill that can be translated into some other area. It won't help you in reading or writing. It won't make you a better baseball player. It just makes you a better games player."

She also ridiculed the idea that games can serve to introduce a youngster to the world of the computer. Sitting in front of a television screen and jiggling a joystick doesn't make for computer literacy, she contended. She compared it to trying to become skilled as an actor, a director, or a producer simply by watching television shows.

After several months of campaigning, Mrs. Lamm was successful in getting the town of Brookhaven to enact permanent legislation to control the games. "Go to the local 7-11," she said, "and you'll see a big sign that says game-playing is not permitted during school hours, and the door to the game room is locked. That's one of our accomplishments."

Mrs. Lamm and her colleagues also prodded local legislators to prohibit the installation of games or the establishing of arcades in close proximity to local schools. Regulations were adopted that mandated that games had to be conspicuously located (so they could be properly supervised); that an adult had to be present at all times when games were in use; and that loitering not be permitted outside the arcades. In addition, license fees were established.

"Some shopkeepers abide by the legislation," Mrs. Lamm said. "But others don't. Nothing is perfect.

"Our concern is with supervision. At one delicatessen, the owner is seldom there. He has sixteen-year-olds slicing ham. How can sixteen-year-olds control ten kids hanging around three machines?"

Foosball World, the principal arcade in Centereach, continued to operate. "Good kids don't go there," Mrs. Lamm said. "Go up to the high school
—they'll tell you. Kids in the honor society, the club people, and football
players—they don't go there.

"I have faith in our teenagers," she declared. "I have faith that they will
make the right judgments. But what about the six- and seven-year olds?
They're not equipped to make the same value judgments. It's these
younger children who need to be protected."

Mrs. Lamm was pleased that the legislation was passed and that the
public was more aware of the video-games problem. "It was a campaign
of awareness," she said. "It was not a hatchet-queen campaign."

With these victories achieved, Mrs. Lamm didn't look upon the games
as any future threat. Interest in the games was declining, she felt. "The
machines aren't being utilized as much as they once were. They're not as
much of a problem as they used to be."

A number of groups supported Mrs. Lamm's claim that the violence
portrayed in some games could have a harmful effect upon children. In the
early 1980s the National Coalition on Television Violence (NCTV) announced it was launching a campaign to combat video-game violence. In
a survey NCTV reported that 89 percent of the games found in arcades had
a violent theme—they featured a player who practiced a weapons skill such
as shooting a gun, rocket, laser, or the like. The organization found 65
percent of all home video games to be of a violent nature, too.

Dr. Thomas Radecki, chairman of the National Coalition on Television
Violence, singled out Berzerk for special criticism. "In this game you're a
stick figure with a handgun," Dr. Radecki stated. "The object is to kill as
many other stick figures as possible, before they kill you. This type of
role-playing practice is certain to have long-term harmful effects on the
player; it teaches violent reactions. These games are training the next
generation of Americans to be even more violent than our current adult
generation, already the most violent in American history."

These criticisms of video games and their effects have been questioned
often, however. There has been a lack of concrete evidence linking video
games and violent behavior.

Peter Favaro, a Long Island, New York, school psychologist was among
those taking an opposing view. "Obviously, the games have aggressive
themes," Mr. Favaro said, "but there is no research to show it translates into
aggressive behavior. If there is aggressive behavior around arcades, that
is not proof of cause and effect. There's aggressive behavior in schools and
around supermarkets, too.

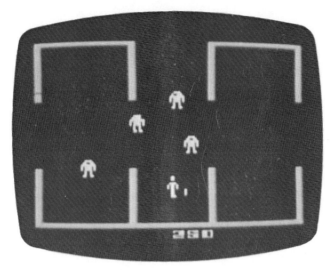

Berzerk—Does it teach violent reactions? (Berzerk is a trademark of Stern Electronics, Inc.)

"In most games, the rules are unclear," Mr. Favaro stated. "You have to project a lot. In Missile Command, for instance, you might be saving a city or participating in a war." In other words, people look upon video games and their plots in different ways.

Don Osborne, vice-president for sales and marketing of coin-operated games for Atari, and the father of a sixteen-year-old daughter and a thirteen-year-old son, also took a stand that's sharply opposed to Mrs. Lamm's. "I don't see the games as threatening at all," Mr. Osborne said. "Young people are a heck of a lot more logical and understanding of the situation than most of the adults who decry video games.

"Perhaps a small percentage—I'd guess less than five percent—are playing the games to an extreme degree. Most have a very wholesome attitude toward the games. They take them in stride. There's been a tremendous amount of distortion as to the amount of involvement young people have in the games. But they're playing as they're doing other things, like reading books, being active in athletics, watching television, and doing their homework. The involvement is not anywhere near what the critics have pointed out."

Mr. Osborne also said: "Where I live—San Jose, California—more and more recreation programs are being taken away from kids because the city can't fund them anymore. The cost of movies, records, and bowling is going up. Video games haven't gone up since 1972.

"It's an exciting, active involvement, an opportunity to extend one's fantasy world. Entertainment, laughing, just being able to have some sort of diversion from the oppression of reality is very necessary. Video games provide that in a special way."

In response to the attacks on video games, Nolan Bushnell told *Video Games* magazine: "I believe it's another case of what I call 'anti-technology' forces at work—the nothings have their say. Whether it's nuclear power or whatever, they're really afraid of technology.

"Also, people have an ingrained notion about leisure—essentially, anything that's fun is somehow not holy.

"What they don't see is that video games are really the training wheels for computer literacy. They almost feel that it's magic that kids can operate computers and they can't. An awful lot of the basic skills that are necessary for computer literacy are learned on computer games. For instance, I don't see any significant difference between moving a race car on a TV screen and moving a cursor [the dot on a computer's video screen that shows where the next character will appear]. These skills are not only allowing kids to become computer literate, but computer skilled."

It's not just arcade games that have attracted criticism. In thousands of homes across the nation where video-game consoles are to be found, parents have expressed concern as to whether these games are harmful to their children's development.

Mrs. Lamm was asked whether she would permit an Atari VCS or other such system to be used in her home. "No," she said emphatically. "We have certain priorities. We're a reading family. We're a talking family. We're a doing family.

"We have priorities as to how we spend our money. My son wants a computer. We're saving to buy him one. My daughter is taking a computer literacy course. If we invest in anything, it will probably be a computer.

"We would rather travel than spend money on games. And I'm big on buying books. My kids know that anytime they want to buy a book, I'll take them to the local bookstore."

Mrs. Lamm had friends who had purchased video-game systems for their homes. "A good friend of mine recently bought an Atari," she said. "But she's sensible. She watches what games are purchased. She limits the amount of time her kids spend playing it. I don't see any problem with that."

As in the case of arcade games, no studies yet exist that give information as to the effect of home video games. "Some people see video games as evil because children aren't necessarily learning when they play," Dr. Michael Lewis, a Rutgers University psychiatrist, told *The New York Times*.

"Yet play for play's sake is valid and useful." Dr. Lewis did express concern, however, that the games did not provide as rich a play experience as some other activities.

Chris Crawford, manager of the Games Research Group at Atari, compared video games to comics. They are both bright and loud, he pointed out; they both involve an intense sensory experience. Neither games or the comics require a very long attention span.

He also compared video games to candy. Like candy, they provide a moment of satisfaction, but little more. Neither has much lasting value.

Video games are probably no better or no worse than candy or the comics. But too much candy can ruin your teeth and reading comics all the time can put a damper on your intellectual development. So, too, a youngster can play video games to excess.

"The chief danger signs for parents to be aware of are children who spend an inordinate amount of time and money on the games," Dr. Robert Millmar, associate professor of psychology at the New York Hospital–Cornell University Medical Center, told the *New York Times*. "If a kid keys on the games as a main reason for living, then he's got real trouble."

9. Today and Tomorrow

Constant change is one of the hallmarks of the video-game industry. In the decade or so after Magnavox introduced Odyssey, one technological advance followed another in quick succession. Many of the innovations took the form of components that could be added on or plugged into the basic game hardware, thus expanding its use. These components included cockpit steering wheels, voice synthesizers, and keyboard add-ons that were able to elevate one's video-game system to the status of a home computer.

Coleco, a company that muscled its way back into the video-game field in the early 1980s (after its adventure with Telstar in the mid-1970s), pioneered many of the advances that took place. Coleco, with its ColecoVi-

---

ColecoVision hardware accepts not only Coleco's cartridges but also, with a special adapter, cartridges put out by Atari and Intellivision. (George Sullivan)

The Intellivoice Voice Synthesis module. (Mattel, Inc.)

sion, was the first company to offer a console with adapters that permitted it to accept cartridges put out by other companies such as Atari or Intellivision. ColecoVision also offered a steering-wheel and gas-pedal attachment for playing Turbo, a popular race-car game.

Mattel Electronics, one of Atari's biggest competitors, introduced Intellivoice in 1982. The Intellivoice Voice Synthesis Model, to use its complete name, plugged into the Intellivision console to be used with special cartridges which produced realistic male and female voices that related to various game situations.

The following year, Mattel began marketing its M Network. This consisted of a device that improved the graphics of Atari's VCS and a library of new Mattel cartridges meant for use with the Atari system. It was almost as if NBC had started producing television shows for presentation on CBS.

Mattel also began marketing a revamped version of Intellivision, called Intellivision II. Interestingly, advances in technology—in chip design and manufacture—permitted Mattel to sell its Intellivision II at a lower retail price than its first Intellivision. Atari's 5200 was that company's new game system for the 1980s. Magnavox unveiled Odyssey[3].

Despite the availability of all the new and spiffy hardware, Atari's VCS —renamed the 2600—continued as the most popular home game system. More VCS units were in use recently than all other home games combined. Atari offered over fifty cartridges for the system and some fifteen software companies also produced VCS cartridges.

A computer keyboard transforms the Atari VCS into a home computer.
(Atari, Inc.)

Besides being involved in the production and marketing of new game hardware and add-on components, most video-game companies were also developing home computers. Such firms as Texas Instruments and Commodore International had flooded the marketplace with small computers for home use. These computers played video games just as well as some of the game consoles. And they cost about the same.

Atari, Mattel, and Coleco were quick to meet this challenge. In 1983 all three companies announced the introduction of keyboards that enabled their game consoles to function as home computers.

"We can no longer talk merely about video games," said Arnold Greenberg, chief executive officer of Coleco. "We should be talking about computerized entertainment, because that is the business Atari is in, and Mattel is in, and Coleco is in."

Just as hardware was improved and became more sophisticated, so it was with software. But first, some background.

Computer memory is measured in bytes. 1,024 bytes, expressed as 1K, is about equal to a single typewritten page. 4K equals 4,096 bytes; 8K 8,192. What are now called "first generation" cartridges—those produced in the mid-to-late 1970s for use with the Atari VCS and by Magnavox for its original Odyssey System—used a 16K microchip, holding 16,384 bytes. These games, with their sticklike figures, were appealing at the time, but there was nothing else available with which to compare them. They were unimaginative by today's standards.

In the early 1980s Intellivision introduced second-generation cartridges with 128K of memory. These were cartridges that Mattel promoted by means of television commercials featuring George Plimpton in which he declared that Intellivision games were "more like the real thing." They were.

ColecoVision, Intellivision II, Odyssey[3], and the Atari 5200 made third-generation cartridges possible. These boasted 256K of working memory, twice as much as any previous cartridge. The results were apparent: brighter and more varied colors, and more sharply drawn figures. The

Controllers available for Atari's VCS. (Atari, Inc.)

sound was clearer and more realistic. There was a more frequent use of music. In addition, game scenarios became more exciting and challenging. Earlier, recall, it was often shoot-shoot-shoot.

Game designers and programmers began selecting game themes and characters from a wide range of sources. Parker Brothers put out cartridges based on Strawberry Shortcake, and Spiderman, the comic-book hero. Atari issued games based on the comic-strip *Peanuts,* assorted Disney characters, and the television's Muppets.

And game manufacturers also discovered Hollywood, or was it the other way around? It doesn't matter. The production of movie-based games became the order of the day, as is evidenced by the following:
- Atari introduced games based on *E.T.* and *Raiders of the Lost Ark.* The company also entered in a joint venture with George Lucas, producer of *Star Wars,* and planned to draw upon his expertise in computer graphics and digital sound to create both arcade and home games, which Atari would then market.
- Sega put a *Star Trek*–inspired game on the market.
- ColecoVision produced a game based on the Tarzan films. The company also hired John Dykstra, who did the special effects for *Star Wars,* to design movielike games.

Improved graphics and realistic game play characterize Atari's newest video game systems. (Atari, Inc.)

Intellivision offers a computer adapter, a computer keyboard, and also a music synthesizer. (Mattel, Inc.)

• Parker Brothers manufactured games based upon *The Empire Strikes Back* and *Return of the Jedi*.

The most notable marriage of video games and the movies involved the motion picture *Tron*. Released by Walt Disney Productions in the summer of 1982, *Tron* told the story of a video-game programmer named Flynn (played by Jeff Bridges), who believes that the company he is working for is marketing his video games without his permission. While doing some clandestine reprogramming of the corporation's computer, Flynn is electronically "sucked" into the circuitry of the computer itself, which is ruled by the Master Control Program, or MCP.

Inside the computer, Flynn and the other digitized warriors are supposed to die fighting on the video-game grid. But Flynn, aided by Tron, manages to thwart the MCP and to break out of the computer world.

At the same time the movie *Tron* was being released to theaters across the country, hundreds of Tron games were being shipped to arcades by Midway. And home versions of Tron—Maze-a-Tron and Tron Deadly Discs —were being readied for nationwide distribution by Mattel.

The arcade version of Tron was extremely popular, and became a staple in the nation's arcades. It actually consisted of four different games in which you, the player, cast in the role of Flynn, battled tanks, light cycles, the MCP cone, and grid bugs.

Tron the movie, was a big disappointment, however. The critics panned

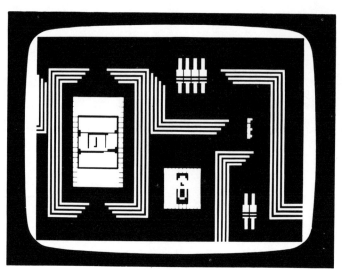

Maze-A-Tron, one of the home versions of Tron. (Mattel, Inc.)

it and the public shunned it. But something remarkable happened. The arcade and home-video versions of Tron continued to zoom in popularity. The youngsters who enjoyed Tron as a video game then began going to the movie.

Disney reissued the film and it attracted more customers than it had the first time. A Disney spokesman admitted that the ticket sales to youngsters who played or bought the video game helped prevent *Tron* from being a box-office failure.

Aside from the Tron game, movie-based video games of the early 1980s were not successful. E.T. sold over a million games, but fell short of expectations. The game based on *Raiders of the Lost Ark* was also a disappointment.

Games with even greater realism in graphics and sound are planned. Games with a three-dimensional quality, which appeared recently, are a step in that direction. Subroc 3-D, from Sega Enterprises, was the first of the 3-D games. Piloting your Subroc craft, you skimmed the ocean in battling seagoing vessels, then soared into the stratosphere to attack spaceships and flying saucers.

In the Subroc 3-D viewing system, a picture for the left eye and one for the right eye are alternately displayed on the monitor screen at the rate of

Spiderman and the Green Goblin, along with Stan Lee, the creator of the two comic book characters, watch the Spiderman video game. (Marvel Comics Group)

thirty images per second. Special shutters for each eye operate in synchronization with the screen images. Looking at the images with both eyes produces a three-dimensional effect.

Games with the technical sophistication of Subroc 3-D are just the

The E.T. game based on the movie was not a big success. (Atari, Inc.)

beginning. The future will bring much more interaction between the player and whatever game he or she happens to be playing. Of course, video games have always been characterized by interaction. When you move the joystick, the character on the screen moves. When you press the fire button, you blast an enemy spaceship. But all of this will be considered quite tame with what is planned.

Tomorrow's games will be ultra-realistic. You may step into a machine that is about the size of a large closet. You will be immediately surrounded by sights and sounds of another world. You could be in outer space, handing the controls of the starship Enterprise. You could be projected back in time; perhaps you will be standing on the flight deck of a World War II aircraft carrier during the Battle of Midway. Or you could be on the playing field during a World Series or Super Bowl.

The wraparound environment is no fantasy. At military bases across the country, the armed services have been employing a new generation of flight simulators using what is called Computer Graphics Imagery to teach gunnery and other wartime skills. Aerial dogfights are so realistic, it's been said, that "players" emerge from the simulators drenched in sweat, their faces drained of color.

This concept recently was introduced to video-game enthusiasts at a unique arcade in San Diego, California. Called the Simutron Tournament Center, it offered consoles in which you played a video game based upon *Star Trek, The Motion Picture,* and that used actual footage from the movie. You sat in a captain's chair wearing a pair of earphones and watching three graphics monitors. Your controls included a joystick and an array of fire buttons.

A quarter was of no use in the Simutron Tournament Center. You rented one of the units for $10 an hour.

Astron Belt, a cockpit-style video game that recently debuted in arcades, was the first interactive game of this type to be offered to the general public. It blended live-action images with computer-generated graphics to produce a space game that visually, at least, rivaled the climactic battle scene in *Star Wars.*

Video disks help to make such games possible. A video disk is a thin, flat, circular plate on which programs and data—pictures and sound—can be stored and played back. Some video disks are created through laser technology. They're played back by means of a low-power laser beam that "reads" information within the disk's "micropits." Because the beam merely glides over the disk without actually touching it—as the needle touches a record when it is being played—there is no wear. The life span of a laser disk can easily exceed that of its owner.

It is generally agreed that comparing video games of today with those of the future is something like comparing the early telegraph with communications satellites. Engineers and designers have dreams on their drawing boards. They're working on turning those dreams into realities. It will happen very quickly.

GLOSSARY

arcade—Any location offering coin-operated entertainment equipment with ten or more video games.

arithmetic logic unit—The area within a computer where information is sorted, calculations performed, and instructions executed.

assembly—A programming language, similar to the English language, that breaks BASIC down into digital codes.

BASIC—A programming language. Basic stands for *Beginners All*-Purpose *S*ymbolic *I*nstruction *C*ode.

bit—An abbreviation for binary digit, one of the two numbers—0 and 1—used to encode computer data. Each bit represents one character in a binary number.

breadboard—An experimental assembly of electronic components for a proposed circuit that is used for testing and evaluating their arrangement.

bug—A mistake in a computer program.

bus—The circuitry that provides for communication between the microprocessor and other electronic elements of a video game.

byte—A unit of memory storage; a byte is made up of a number of bits, usually eight.

cartridge—A self-contained magnetic tape unit containing a game program.

central processing unit—The microchip that controls a video game.

chip—A small piece of silicon upon which a complete integrated circuit has been etched.

coin-op—A video game that is operated by a coin, usually a quarter or a token; short for coin-operated.

computer language—Any group of letters, numbers, or other symbols that enables an individual to instruct or otherwise communicate with a computer.

debugging—The process of finding errors in a computer program.

dedicated microprocessor—A microprocessor that has been designed to do a specific job, and cannot be programmed by the user.

digitize—To render characters or graphics into digits, or into a binary system that is understandable to the computer.

disk drive—The device that operates or drives the connection between the computer and a disk.

floppy disk—A flexible plastic disk upon which information is stored for computer generation.

hardware—The game console, as opposed to the "software," or cartridges.

input—The point where the player communicates with the game's central processing unit. Input can be transmitted by a joystick, paddles, or a keyboard.

integrated circuit—A tiny slice of silicon or germanium that holds thousands of transistors, capacitors, and other electronic components.

joystick—A knob or control stick common to video games.

K—Stands for 1,024 bits of computer memory. A 64K memory can store 65,536 bits of information (64 × 1,024).

language—A set of statements used to instruct a computer.

memory chip—A semiconductor device that stores information in the form of electrical charges.

microprocessor—The central chip that controls all of the functions of a video game or home computer.

output—The information that appears on the video screen after the game's various electronic elements have processed the input.

program—A set of instructions that causes a computer to carry out a specific operation.

RAM (random access memory)—Computer or game memory in which pieces of information are held only temporarily.

random event generator—A device that provides for a degree of unpredictability in the game program.

raster—A graphics display system, the type common to color television, in which images are created by the firing of electrons at the tiny bits of phosphor that coat the back of the screen.

ROM (read only memory)—Computer or game memory in which information is permanently fixed during the manufacturing process. Game cartridges are ROM.

software—The game cartridge, or any program that can be played on a game console.

street location—Any video-game location with less than ten games.

transistor—An electronic device that can act as a switch or amplifier. A silicon chip may contain many thousands of transistors.

vacuum tube—An electron tube used in the circuitry of early radios, television sets, and other telecommunications devices.

VCS—Short for Video Computer System; the console manufactured by Atari that accepts game cartridges produced by the company and other manufacturers.

vector graphics—A graphics display system in which images are created by a vector that draws lines to form shapes which can have a three-dimensional quality.

INDEX